M000232662

THE PARATROOPER TRAINING POCKET MANUAL 1939–45

Edited by Chris McNab

CASEMATE
Oxford & Philadelphia

Published in Great Britain and
the United States of America in 2019 by
CASEMATE PUBLISHERS
The Old Music Hall, 106–108 Cowley Road, Oxford OX4 1JE, UK
1950 Lawrence Road, Havertown, PA 19083, USA

Introduction and chapter introductory texts by Chris McNab
© Casemate Publishers 2019

Hardback Edition: ISBN 978-1-61200-791-5
Digital Edition: ISBN 978-1-61200-792-2

A CIP record for this book is available from the British Library

Printed in the Czech Republic by FINIDR, s.r.o.

Typeset in India for Casemate Publishing Services.
www.casematepublishingservices.com

The information contained in the documents in this book is solely for historical interest
and does not constitute advice. The publisher accepts no liability for the consequences of
following any of the details in this book.

For a complete list of Casemate titles, please contact:

CASEMATE PUBLISHERS (UK)
Telephone (01865) 241249
Fax (01865) 794449
Email: casemate-uk@casematepublishers.co.uk
www.casematepublishers.co.uk

CASEMATE PUBLISHERS (US)
Telephone (610) 853-9131
Fax (610) 853-9146
Email: casemate@casematepublishers.com
www.casematepublishers.com

Image credits: Pages 23, 31, 35, 39, 56, 58, 60, 61, 62, 64, 107, 108, 110, 113 and 118:
          National Archives. AIR 10/3845
          Pages 70, 72 and 74: AIR 10/2968

CONTENTS

INTRODUCTION

World War II was a conflict replete with *in extremis* innovation, both tactical and technical. Although the seeds of many of these innovations had been sown in World War I and the inter-war years, it was between 1939 and 1945 that warfare truly emerged into the modern era. The steps forward range from the incremental to the profound, and included either the invention, or the advancement, of wireless communications, mechanised and armoured warfare, monoplane combat aviation (not least the advent of jet aircraft), guided weaponry, carrier combat and atomic bombs, to name just a few of the big-hitters. But a salient addition to this list is surely the proven advent of airborne warfare.

Parachute Potential

Although the origins of parachuting actually go back to the 18th century (possibly even back to ancient times, depending on how you frame the chronology), it was in the early 20th century that parachuting as we understand it truly emerged. A formative influence was American inventor Charles Broadwick, who as a 13-year-old boy in the late 1800s dazzled spectators by performing parachute jumps from hot-air balloons. His parachutes were at this stage large muslin canopies, hanging loose and open beneath the balloon, with a trapeze for the parachutist to grasp in the descent. In 1906, however, Broadwick made a seminal leap forward, by packing both the parachute and its lines into a backpack; a static line connecting the balloon and the pack deployed the parachute at a safe distance from the balloon's basket. In one key moment, Broadwick had invented the type of parachute system that still dominates much of the sport, and airborne warfare, to this day.

Even as Broadwick, and soon others, pushed parachute technology onwards, some innovative individuals in the military were starting to think about the marriage between parachutes and aviation. The first true powered and controlled flight by a heavier-than-air aircraft had only taken just taken place, in December 1903, courtesy of Orville and Wilbur Wright and their *Wright Flyer*, but by the end of the first decade of the 20th century aviation was already being considered as a tool with military potential. Parachutes offered both civilian and military aviators a way of escaping a damaged or defective aircraft spiralling down to destruction. On 1 March 1912, US Army captain Albert Berry made history's first parachute jump from a fixed-wing aircraft, a Benoist 'pusher' aircraft flying over Jefferson Barracks in St Louis, Missouri. Yet although parachutes were quickly revealed as a safety asset for aviators – especially with further innovations such as the invention of the ripcord (which allowed aircrew to deploy their parachutes at a safe distance from the aircraft) – during World War I they were almost never worn by the pilots and crews of fixed-wing aircraft, for a mixture of cultural and practical reasons. (They were used by the crews of observation balloons, which were extremely vulnerable to being destroyed by both ground fire and aircraft attack.) At the very end of the war in 1918, however, the Deutsche Luftstreitkräfte (German Air Force) introduced the first standard issue air force parachute, courtesy of a design by Otto Heinecke, who worked as ground crew on airships.

It was during the inter-war years, however, that parachutes progressively became standard-issue equipment amongst the world's air forces. Also in the 1920s and 1930s, a new breed of military thinkers began to think more ambitiously about what parachutes and aircraft could offer not to aerial combatants, but rather the foot-slogging infantry. Land warfare was about to acquire a vertical dimension.

The Airborne Concept

Before resuming our history, it is worth clarifying some core concepts about airborne warfare. Strictly speaking, 'airborne' can be used to refer to three types of aerial deployment. The first is by parachute, a body of paratroopers being deployed direct to a 'drop zone' (DZ) from a passing aircraft. Paratroop operations offer a mix of advantages and vulnerabilities. The most important advantage is that a potentially very large force of infantry can be deployed not only over major obstacles (rivers, mountains, frontline fortifications etc.), but also into enemy rear areas largely well protected against ground force advance. The paratroopers would also tend to arrive with a heavy dose of surprise; enemy troops occupying 'safe' rear areas would rarely be psychologically or practically prepared to fight a major battle in an instant. Once dropped and in action, the paratroopers could thereafter perform a tactically useful range of missions – cutting enemy supply lines; seizing and holding high-value targets; destabilising enemy offensive or defensive operations; reinforcing surrounded or otherwise cut off allied units; tying up enemy forces even as other allied units make a ground offensive.

On the debit side, it is the very expeditious nature of paratroopers that makes them so exposed to possible catastrophic defeat. Paratroopers go into action only with the equipment they can carry – largely just small-arms, ammunition, water and basic rations – or which can be parachuted in containers (little heavier than a mortar or recoilless rifle, although sometimes light vehicles and heavier artillery pieces were dropped). This fact makes them almost incapable of sustained operations; paratroopers usually rely upon a ground advance reaching them before they are overwhelmed by local enemy forces, who will steadily recover from the shock of the airborne landing and will respond with gathering strength.

When the airborne principle works, great victories are to be had, as demonstrated by the Germans during their operations in the Netherlands and Belgium in May 1940. When it doesn't, the consequences can be profound for the isolated and weakening paratroopers – here the disastrous, epic Anglo-American Operation *Market Garden* in the Netherlands in September 1944 stands out, which resulted in the near-destruction of the British 1st Airborne Division around Arnhem and Oosterbeek after the failed overland advance of XXX Corps.

The paratrooper's precarious lot was, and remains, the key reason why most airborne troops are regarded as occupying the elite end of the military spectrum. Airborne soldiers must be physically hardened to cope with intensive, self-reliant combat; their leaders have to be daring, inventive and disdainful of adversity. But paratroopers also have to own the intelligence to master the skills of parachuting and advanced infantry tactics; as we shall see in the manuals presented in Chapter 1, the syllabus requirements for paratroopers were extremely demanding, hence the high drop-out rate during training.

The other two strands of airborne warfare during World War II were glider deployment and airlanding. The former utilized towed, then released, gliders to make silent approaches to landing zones (LZs), the aircraft offering the means to deliver heavier equipment (e.g. vehicles and more substantial artillery pieces) while also landing a landing body of troops with less dispersal (hopefully). Airlanding, by contrast, involved the landing of troops in powered transport aircraft directly into the combat zone, usually on a secured airfield and typically as follow-up reinforcements for the vanguard troops. (Both forms of deployment will be explained in more detail in the subsequent chapters.)

The three forms of airborne deployment offered the tacticians of World War II a new dimension in warfare, quite literally. The airborne soldiers broke apart some of the old tactical restrictions of frontline, terrain and frontiers, although it would take judicious commanders to ensure that they were not just unnecessary sacrifices made a long way from reinforcements.

The Rise of the Airborne Forces

Practical parachute experiments and minor airlifting operations become viable in the 1920s – Britain's airlifting of a battalion of troops from Egypt to Iraq in 1923 is a key example – but it was during the 1930s that the world's most militarized nations truly began the airborne age. The Soviets were particular pioneers in this field, forming both airlanded and parachute regiments and brigades, and conducting aerial movements on a major scale – an exercise in 1935 saw 3,000 paratroopers plus 8,000 airlanded troops deployed – and their subsequent growth was prodigious. By mid 1941, the Red Army had no fewer than five airborne corps, of divisional strength, rising to 10 by the end of the year. Yet having taken an early lead, the Soviets backtracked in 1942, converting the 10 corps to guards rifle divisions –

essentially foot infantry. This largely became the lot of most Soviet airborne forces during the war, although they were held in high regard as elite ground troops.

Probably the most significant outcome of the Soviets' early explorations of airborne warfare lay not in what they ultimately achieved, but what they inspired others to do. German observers of the Russian exercises took the lessons back home, and in a rapidly militarizing Germany – from 1933 under Hitler's leadership and free from the structural and material limitations of the Versailles Treaty – the exciting concept of an elite airborne force progressively took hold, at least amongst the German Air Force. In 1935 Hermann Göring, head of the Luftwaffe, formed a single parachute battalion from the Landespolizei paramilitary police he also governed, as Prussian Minister of the Interior. In 1938, this seed became I Battalion/ Fallschirmjäger Regiment (FJR) 1, the regiment acquiring a second battalion the following year. In July 1938, the 7. Flieger Division was created, which by 1940 had authority over three *Fallschirmjäger* regiments (FJR 1, FJR 2 and FJR 3). The German Army, seeing itself left behind, began developing airlanding units in the late 1930s; the airlanding concept had been operationally proven during the Spanish Civil War (1936–39), when Nationalists used German-manufactured Junkers Ju-52 transporters to shift thousands of troops from North Africa to Spain. The key formation to emerge was the 22. (Luftlande) Infantry Division, formed as a regular infantry division in 1935 but trained in airlanding operations from 1938. Although the 22. Division would remain an army formation (much to Göring's annoyance), the 7. Flieger Division, and later XI. Fliegerkorps would work closely alongside army airlanding capability.

Little used in Germany's 1939 campaign in Poland, the elite *Fallschirmjäger* began to earn their combat reputation in Norway and Denmark in 1940, where they were principally applied for bridge and airfield seizures. But it was the stunning glider-borne operation to capture the major Belgian fortress of Eben Emael on 10 May 1940 that changed everything. Landing silently in DFS 230 gliders, and armed with little more than small arms and special shaped-charge demolitions, a few dozen paratroopers defeated a fortress garrison of more than 650 men. In much the same way as the SAS found themselves catapulted into the public imagination following the 1980 Iranian Embassy siege action, the *Fallschirmjäger* took an almost superhero status.

Such was the belief in the *Fallschirmjäger*, that on 20 May 1941, virtually the whole of XI. Fliegerkorps, plus airlanding forces, was used for the invasion of Crete. Nearly 10,000 paratroopers were dropped on the first day alone (17,530 by 23 May), but although the Germans were eventually victorious, the casualty rates were horrific – nearly 7,000 men were killed. The consequent disillusionment with the *Fallschirmjäger*'s tactical possibilities meant that for the remainder of the war they were largely used as ground forces, although admittedly elite ones, meaning they were sent to some of the worst parts of the fronts until the end of the war and suffered disproportionate casualties as a result.

Germany's European Axis partner, Italy, also had parachute forces, raising the first such units in Italian-governed Libya in March 1938. Yet the growth and utility of the Italian airborne forces was always limited. Its apogee was the 1st Folgore Parachute Division, formed in February 1942, but this was wiped out in North Africa in the autumn of 1942.

In Britain, meanwhile, the immediate aftermath of the Allied defeat in France saw an inspired Winston Churchill give the order, on 6 June 1940, to form a parachute force within the British Army, up to 5,000 men strong. This force emerged in slow and halting increments, beginning with the establishment of the Central Landing Establishment and School at RAF Ringway, which acted as a centre for recruitment and training. The first official parachute unit was No. 2 Commando, formed in battalion strength in July 1940, and this was subsequently redesignated the 11th Special Air Service Battalion, then (September 1941) the 1st Parachute Battalion, which contained both paratroopers and glider troops. Expansion continued apace, an airlanding brigade and a parachute brigade formed into the 1st Airborne Division in November 1941; a second parachute brigade would be added in July 1942. Eventually, 17 battalions of paratroopers were formed by the Parachute Regiment. These battalions were divided into the 1st and 6th Airborne Divisions and the 2nd Independent Parachute Brigade Group.

The British airborne forces fought with distinction across numerous theatres – Burma, India, North Africa, Sicily, Italy – although they are primarily remembered for the major airborne actions in support of the D-Day landings in Normandy on 6 June 1944, conducted by the 6th Airborne Division, and the ill-fated Arnhem operation mentioned above. The failure of the Arnhem action was largely one of strategy, not of the tactical ability of the British paratroopers, however, and Axis forces rightly came to fear these men who wore the red beret.

Like Britain, the United States came haltingly to the promise of airborne forces, but eventually was to wield airborne formations of unrivalled scale and power. Small-scale parachute units were activated in 1940, including the 1st Parachute Battalion (later 501st Parachute Battalion) in September 1940, and by the end of 1941 the number of battalions had risen to four. Under the pressures of war, however, the US Airborne forces would eventually come to possess five airborne divisions – the 11th, 13th, 17th, 82nd and 101st – each containing paratrooper and glider regiments, plus a host of other divisions capable of airlanding operations.

US airborne troops were first committed to action in October 1942, when soldiers of the 509th Parachute Infantry Regiment (PIR) made combat drops during the Allied invasion of French North Africa, Operation *Torch*. Subsequently the airborne forces were much used across the Mediterranean and European Theatres of Operation; alongside the British airborne forces, they also performed their largest missions during the D-Day landings in Normandy and as a key part of Operation *Market Garden*. The 101st Airborne was also lauded for its dogged ground defence of Bastogne, besieged by the Germans during their Ardennes offensive of December 1944–January 1945. We should remember that US paratroopers served in the Pacific also, such as in the 11th Airborne Division's major combat operations over the Philippines, which would ultimately cost the division more than 2,400 casualties.

The Pacific theatre also witnessed the deployment of Japanese paratroopers. The airborne concept was well-suited to Japan's plans for a rapid imperial conquest across a vast expanse of often inaccessible territories, although the difficult terrain of many of those territories limited the possibilities of safe parachute drops. Unusually, both the Japanese Army and the Imperial Japanese Navy formed airborne units, which subsequently made combat jumps over the Dutch East Indies in early 1942. From late 1942, however, Japan found itself locked largely into an escalating, desperate defence of its shrinking empire, and hence the opportunities for major airborne operations rarely presented themselves again.

Airborne Doctrine

As airborne warfare was so new in World War II, both in concept and in practice, the manuals presented in this volume show doctrine at its formative stage. They come from a range of mainly British and American sources, plus US intelligence assessments of the much-respected *Fallschirmjäger*. Much of their focus is concerned with how to achieve the right blend of equipment and tactics, plus ways of negotiating the fundamental challenge of all airborne ops – how to put paratroopers down in the right place at the right time, a challenge simple in description but irreducibly complex in practice. There was also the underlying concern with survivability, as it was recognised that from the moment they landed, airborne troops were fighting a losing battle against the clock, unless they could eventually be relieved or reinforced. At every level, airborne operations stretched mind, body and courage, and it is little wonder that airborne units were composed of such exceptional men.

CHAPTER I

RECRUITMENT AND TRAINING

From the outset, it was recognised by all World War II's combatants that paratroopers were to a breed apart. Not only did they need to acquire a highly specialist and dangerous skill – parachute jumping – but they also had to possess heightened physical fitness, superb tactical awareness and fluent weapons handling if they were to survive the engagements around and beyond the DZ. For this reason, the recruitment and training programmes for airborne troops tended to be more punishing, and more attentive to character traits, than many regular infantry units.

Recruits to the airborne were almost invariably volunteers, not unwilling conscripts. They tended to join out of a sense of adventure and a desire to 'be the best', aided by the glamorous marketing of the airborne forces on film and in the print media. Some of the volunteers might also already be serving soldiers, requesting the transfer for advancement and action. Once they had passed the initial battery of medical, fitness and psychological tests, the recruits embarked upon a lengthy programme of instruction. At most fundamental, this training was broken down into two core phases: basic training and airborne training – we often refer to the latter as 'jump school'.

We can illustrate this process by looking at the typical training programme for a US airborne soldier. The basic training stage usually lasted 13 weeks (training programmes might be a little more compressed later in the war) and was largely similar in content to the basic training of the US infantry, albeit with higher physical intensity and more exacting benchmarks for failure. The first weeks of basic training revolved around introducing the men to the fundamentals of military life (uniform, etiquette, barracks procedures, etc.) while also pushing them to the limits of their endurance with PT and route marches. As the weeks progressed, however, they would switch focus more to infantry tactical skills and weapon handling, bolstered by classroom instruction. The paratrooper training, known as 'Basic Airborne', lasted four weeks and was conducted at Fort Benning, Georgia. It was separated into four phases, each of a week's duration: Week 1 – physical training; Week 2 – parachute theory and introduction to training equipment; Week 3 – packing a parachute and advanced ground training, using a wide variety of specialist equipment; Week 4 – five real parachute jumps, including a night jump. If the recruit survived all four weeks, and successfully made all five jumps, without hesitation, he was awarded his wings.

The text in this chapter is, however, from a British source, the extensive *Parachute Training Manual* (1944). It provides, in great detail, some of the elements that went into producing the finished paratrooper, including what the instructors looked for in the recruit's psychological make-up. Although it is squarely focused on the British airborne process, it is representative of many of the airborne training programmes of this time.

From *Parachute Training Manual* (1944)

INTRODUCTION

1. The instructional or training section of a Parachute Training School is by far the most important section of the school, and all other sections must be subordinate to it. Its tasks are summarised as follows:—

    (i) *To Instil into Pupils the Will to Jump*
        This is perhaps its most difficult task as it requires a knowledge and understanding of the pupil's character and mental problems.

    (ii) *To Teach Pupils how to Parachute*
        How to jump, to descend and to land. This is a physical requirement which can be taught, provided the necessary mental attitude exists.

    (iii) *To Instruct Pupils in Various Associated Subjects*
        The care and handling of parachutes, aircraft drill and discipline, etc. These three main tasks are discussed in greater detail below.

The Will to Jump

2. The act of parachuting, which involves throwing oneself into space, is not a natural act. At the same time, since the adoption of the parachute by the Army as a means of transport, many hundreds of people are jumping to earth every day by parachute. It is the task of a Parachute Training School to make pupils look upon this new means of conveyance as a simple and normal performance, and not as a daring stunt of which only exceptional men are capable. With the present generation this is not always an easy task, since the parachute is still comparatively new and has an aura of black magic in the same way as the motorcar and the telephone had for the Victorians.

The problem will become much easier as the next generation grows up, since it is more likely to look upon parachuting in the same light as the present younger generation looks upon flying.

But, for the present, it must be realised that those undergoing training are necessarily under considerable nervous and mental strain throughout their course, and consideration and allowance should be made for this fact in laying down the instructional system.

3. Until the time arrives when a descent by parachute will be looked upon as no more unusual or hazardous than a descent in a lift or funicular railway, the best advice that can be given for creating the right attitude of mind is as follows:—

    (i) The pupils must be made exceptionally fit physically. This will create mental determination, confidence and high morale.

    (ii) Complete confidence in the parachute, and in all ancillary equipment and personnel, must be instilled into pupils.

(iii) It is equally important to inculcate an attitude of respect. As in flying, over-confidence is as dangerous as over-anxiety. A middle path of care and respect for the parachute itself, for the exit, for the descent and for the landing, during training and after three, ten, and even fifty descents, should be stressed and always maintained.

(iv) An atmosphere of healthy enthusiasm is necessary throughout all sections of the school.

(v) There must always be a good object for every jump; and this means that the object must be considered a good one by the paratroop, as well as by the spectator or staff officer who is witnessing, or may have ordered, the descent. At an initial training school this problem is overcome by ordering a specific exercise after each descent, graduated from a simple report by the parachutist to a member of the instructional staff to a definite paratroop exercise after the final training descent.

(vi) The more jumping that takes place, the easier and better it is for everyone. Experience shows it is comparatively easy to jump when hundreds of others are doing so around one, but it involves a much greater effort to jump by oneself. At a school therefore, it is advisable to intersperse courses so that one is on the initial training phase and another on its jumping course.

(vii) A useful factor with pupils has been found to be the thought that "as thousands have done it before me, I must be capable of doing it."

(viii) The avoidance at all cost of boredom, waiting about and conditions of cold, before jumping.

These are a few practical considerations which have been found to be useful at a school. But a good deal remains to be learnt about the possibility of inculcating the will to jump in doubtful cases which, whilst largely a question of morale, may also be due to causes where medical advice can be of assistance.

This problem assumes much greater importance in advanced training where the whole question of jumping, and refusal to jump, is likely to be more difficult than at a school.

How to Jump

The task under this heading is to teach pupils the art of parachuting which involves:—

(i) Correct and rapid exit. This is necessary to ensure the proper functioning of the parachute; and, when team jumping, to ensure short sticks on the ground.

(ii) Correct attitude and control during the descent. This is a prerequisite for a good landing.

(iii) Correct landing technique. This is necessary to avoid injury, particularly when wearing full equipment and when landing in conditions of wind.

To achieve these objects extreme physical fitness, and particularly suppleness, are required. An alert and disciplined body and mind will result in correct and rapid exits; good arm muscles are needed for control of the parachute during descent, whilst sound leg, neck and back muscles are required to ensure a safe landing. But physical fitness by itself is not enough.

There is a right and a wrong way of doing things. If a pupil performs in the right way, he should not hurt himself; if he performs in the wrong way, he probably will. For this reason parachuting can be termed an art. The amount of skill required is not great, but a certain minimum standard is essential for success.

[. . .]

THE PUPIL AND THE INSTRUCTOR

The Pupil

6. Experience has shown that physical fitness, common sense, and character are the foundations from which a successful paratroop can be built. Any normal soldier who possesses these attributes and the physical requirements is suitable. It is true that men over the age of 35, a height of 6 ft. and a weight of 13 stone have proved more liable to injury than younger, shorter and lighter men; and it may not be economic in their own, or in military interests, to train them. But there are many exceptions amongst these older and heavier men, and the right policy is to judge each individual case on its own merits, according to the physical and mental condition of the man and his value as a specialist. Amongst younger men, the light and short man appears the ideal, provided he possesses sufficient strength and stamina.

7. It has been the practice in England for paratroops to be volunteers, and as long as this policy provides all the numbers required, it clearly has advantages. The instructional system must aim at ensuring that every pupil, so long as he is physically fit, is rendered determined enough by the middle of the course to jump, and by the end of the course to jump successfully with full equipment. This is no easy task when numbers are large and pupils are drawn from all sources and classes, but the individual instructional system outlined later in this section has been designed to achieve this object.

8. In selecting paratroops, character (used in the sense of mental and physical self-control and strength rather than a clean crime record) is as important as physical standards. The general qualities required are those possessed by any normal man; but in particular they must include the ability to conquer doubt and fear, and the determination and will power to trust the parachute and oneself. Nervous and hesitant individuals are unsuitable for training as parachutists. Jumping will always involve some emotional strain, even when the individual has made many descents, and willingness and determination to bear and overcome this strain are necessary. It is therefore evident that medical opinion can be of value in helping to select those best fitted for parachuting.

9. *Refusals.*—At various stages of training refusals to continue training or to jump will occur. Sometimes one individual refuses alone; sometimes several at a time. It is necessary to distinguish between refusals due to an abnormal fear of heights or of flying, and refusals due to lack of the necessary moral fibre. A pupil can be turned into a refusal case unnecessarily owing to an unsatisfactory introduction to heights or to flying. If a pupil refuses to jump, experience shows that this is a feeling which he will in all probability never overcome, and the best policy is not to give him a second chance. It is in advisable to cajole or persuade him beyond normal encouragement. The reasons for refusals are, of course, many and varied.

Typical reasons are:—

   (i) Lack of the necessary moral fibre.

  (ii) Excessive fear (either of falling, injury or death).

 (iii) Domestic reasons (wife or family objections).

It is best for the pupil to be withdrawn from the course and from the school as soon as possible, lest his action should infect his fellow pupils. The pupil himself by loss of self respect is usually the greatest sufferer.

The Instructor

10. A very high standard of instructor is required since he is the key to the success of any Parachute Training School. The whole system after the initial toughening stage is based on individual instruction. Each instructor has a small section such as ten pupils under his charge and he takes them through their course from beginning to end. Under this system the instructor takes a personal interest in each individual man and gets to know him well. In this way he can best gain the pupils' confidence and help them in their difficulties. It is not unlike the system adopted for teaching pilots to fly and has been found very satisfactory in practice. The attributes required of instructors are:—

   (i) *Personality.*—The instructor must possess personality if he is to command respect and inspire confidence.

  (ii) *Instructional ability.*—The instructor must possess the ability to teach, because unless he is interested in teaching in itself, his enthusiasms will quickly tire. He must become a teacher of the highest class since he has to understand and influence the characters and minds of his pupils in addition to teaching them physical exercises.

 (iii) *Ability to parachute.*—An instructor must be able and willing to jump and demonstrate whenever required. Experience has shown that whilst many instructors enjoy jumping themselves, they find it a far greater strain to make other people jump and be responsible for their safety.

 (iv) *Endurance.*—The physical and mental strain of teaching pupils course after course, frequently at dawn and dusk, and sometimes at night, is considerable, and a sense of humour, confidence and stamina are all essential.

(v) *Enthusiasm.*—An instructor must possess this attribute both to inspire his pupils and to maintain his own interest in his work.

(vi) *Sense of responsibility.*—This is a necessary attribute since the instructor is absolutely responsible for his pupil from the time of his entry until the time of his departure, either as a qualified parachutist, or returned to his unit unqualified through injury, refusal, or other reason. A special sense of responsibility is required during the jumping phase, for it can truly be said that the instructor has the lives and well-being of his pupils in his hands; he must steady the nervous, radiate confidence by his own attitude, and ensure the safety of all by his attention to every detail of their equipment.

OUTLINE OF THE TRAINING SYLLABUS

11. The total length of the Paratroop Training Course in wartime has been fixed at six weeks, the first three of which are devoted to military training under Army Control, and the last three to parachute training under R.A.F. Control.

The whole course is divided into phases as follows:—

(i) Selection and Toughening Training—2 weeks—Army Control.

(ii) Battle School Training—1 week—Army Control.

(iii) Synthetic Ground Training—1 week—R.A.F. Control.

(iv) Practical Parachuting—2 weeks—R.A.F. Control.

NOTE:—The periods are approximate only, and periods (iii) and (iv) will necessarily overlap each other.

A more detailed analysis of the phases is as follows:—

Selection and Toughening Training, etc.

12. As the administrative work to be undertaken and subjects to be taught during this period are matters directly concerning the military authorities, it is convenient that the Army should control this part of the training. The subjects to be covered in this initial stage are tabulated thus:—

(i) *Administration*
   (a) Assembly and clear statement as to the requirements of a paratroop.
   (b) Recording and grouping.

(ii) *Medical*
   (a) Medical examination—fitness decision.
   (b) Dental examination and treatment.
   (c) Psychological assessment—intelligence tests, etc.

(iii) *Theoretical Instruction*
   (a) Morale building lectures, stimulation of interest in parachuting, etc.
   (b) Lectures on Airborne Forces from the Army aspect, etc.

(iv) *Practical Instruction*
    (a) Military training
    (b) Physical conditioning and toughening exercises.
    (c) Air experience (if practicable).
    (d) Instruction in supply dropping apparatus and in airborne and foreign weapons.
    (e) Acclimatisation to heights (Trainasium).

NOTE:—It will be noticed that this syllabus does not include any elementary instruction in parachuting, since this is an R.A.F. responsibility included under the second phase. Where circumstances permit, however, it would be advantageous to include such instruction at this initial stage if R.A.F. Instructors are available.

Battle School Training

13. For further details see para. 26.

Synthetic Ground Training

14. At this, the second half of the course, the R.A.F. takes charge of the training and teaches on the ground by means of Synthetic Apparatus, the main principles of parachuting and other ancillary subjects. The time required for this phase depends largely on the physical and mental condition of the trainees on arrival. The period is between 5 and 10 days, according to circumstances.

The subjects covered under this heading are tabulated below:—

THEORETICAL INSTRUCTION—(Lectures)

(i) *Primary Lectures*
    The Parachute.
    Parachuting.
    The use of Training Apparatus.
    Exit Technique.
    Control in the Air.
    Landing Technique.
    Aircraft Drill and Containers.
    Oral Questionnaire.

(ii) *Films*
    General Interest Films on Parachuting.
    Instructional Films on Parachuting.

PRACTICAL INSTRUCTION

(i) PHYSICAL TRAINING

P.T. Exercises.
Games—field and minor.
Swimming.

(ii) GROUND TRAINING

   (a) *Exit Training using* the following apparatus:—

     Mock Aperture.

     Fuselage.

     High Aperture.

     Moving Aperture.

     Air Brake.

   (b) *Control in the Air* using:—

     The Turning Trainer.

     The Harness Swing.

     The Oscillation Swing.

     The Winch.

   (c) *Landing Training* using the following apparatus:—

     The Fall Trainer and Harness Fall Trainer.

     The Slide.

     Landing Trainers.

     Ropes.

     The "Giant Stride."

     The Winch.

     The Bomb-release gear swing.

     The Air Brake.

     The Overhead Railway.

   (d) *Tower Descents (Controlled)*

   (e) *Harness Release and Dragging*

   (f) *Fitting and Handling of Parachute*

   (g) *Aircraft Drill on School type aircraft*

     Aircraft Drill.

     Emplaning Drill.

     Take off, travel and action stations. Stropping up.

Stick Exits.

Abandoning Aircraft.

Container loading.

NOTE:—There should be much repetition use of the Synthetic apparatus after Practical Parachuting has commenced, during the 5th and 6th weeks of the Course.

Practical Parachuting

15. It is not usually possible, owing to weather conditions, to fix a timetable for the fourth phase of training, but the number of Parachute Descents included in the present syllabus is EIGHT, and the subjects to be covered are tabulated thus:—

THEORETICAL INSTRUCTION—(Lectures)

(i) *Advanced Lectures*

History of Parachuting.

Foreign methods of Parachuting.

Manually operated Parachute.

Further aspects of landing technique.

Airborne Operations.

Aircraft and Gliders.

Supply dropping apparatus.

Questionnaire (Oral).

(ii) *Advanced Films*

General interest films on Airborne Exercises and Operations.

Instructional Films on Parachuting.

PRACTICAL INSTRUCTION

(i) *Watching and Discussing descents*

(ii) *Air Jumps in the following sequence:*

Jump No. 1. Captive Balloon—from 700 ft.

Jump No. 2. Captive Balloon—from 700 ft.

Jump No. 3. Aircraft Jump—slow pair from 800 ft.

Jump No. 4. Aircraft Jump—slow five from 600–800 ft.

Jump No. 5. Aircraft Jump—section of ten from 600–800 ft. (Containers on the ground.)

Jump No. 6. Aircraft Jump—section of ten from 600–700 ft. (Section exercise with containers and, arms dropped from aircraft, followed by D.Z. drill.)

Jump No. 7. Aircraft Jump—three sections of ten from 3 aircraft in formation from 600 ft. (Platoon exercise with containers and arms dropped from aircraft, followed by exercise.)

Jump No. 8. Captive Balloon—NIGHT descent from 700 ft. (Any time after 4th descent.)

(iii) *Instructional Discussions*

Discussion and Corrective training after each descent.

(iv) *Aircraft Drill* on various fuselages

Emplaning.

Take-off, travelling and action stations

Stropping up.

Stick exits.

(v) *Containers*

Packing.

Loading.

(vi) *Physical Training*

Exercises.

Games.

Cross-country running.

Tactical marches.

(vii) *Outdoor Recreation*

Climbing and falling.

Obstacle Course.

(viii) *Dragging Practice*

(ix) *Water Descents* (if required).

Packing and Maintenance of Parachutes

16. It has not been the practice in England for paratroops to pack their own parachutes. Their parachutes are packed by special R.A.F. personnel.

If each pupil is to learn to pack and maintain his own parachute, extra time and space for instruction would be needed, and in wartime this has not been considered necessary. But it is clearly desirable, if training facilities and time exist, for each paratroop to be capable of packing a parachute. If this instruction is to be given, about one more week would have to be added to the training period, bringing the total training time to seven weeks.

The instruction could be spaced over the R.A.F. period of the training, and if the pupil is taught to pack his own parachute, it is a good system for the paratroop to use the same parachute throughout his course. This will teach him to take care of it and take an interest in it. If pupils do not pack their own parachutes, it is usual to issue parachutes in rotation.

SELECTION, TOUGHENING AND BATTLE SCHOOL TRAINING

17. Three weeks or a little longer is devoted to this part of the course. It is inadvisable to shorten this period, otherwise there is not sufficient time to carry out the selection tests and training necessary to ensure that the trainee possesses the right type of character to make a paratroop. The training of a paratroop is expensive, and it is most important to weed out unsatisfactory individuals during the early stages of training rather than later.

The work to be carried out during this preliminary period is as follows:—

Administration

18. (i) *Assembly and Enunciation of the Qualities required of a Paratroop.*— Although the duties of a paratroop will have been made clear to soldiers before their arrival for selection, the assembly on intake provides an excellent opportunity for reiterating and clarifying these duties. It is so important for a high standard to be demanded and attained, that the men must be imbued with the ideals of airborne troops from the beginning of their training. The highest standard of morale must pervade the camp, and a recruit must feel privileged to have obtained entry rather than given the impression he is a daredevil, to be thanked and praised for taking grave risk.

(ii) *Recording and Grouping.*—Scrupulous attention to correct recording of intakes, grading of pupils, examination of individuals and documents, together with kitting, housing and feeding, will do much to put the prospective trainee in a receptive frame of mind.

Medical

19. Medical examination, dental treatment night vision tests, and such psychological tests as are deemed necessary should be carried out with care. Time spent by experienced inspectors and examiners will be rewarded by the maintenance of a high standard of entrant.

Theoretical Instruction

20. (i) Morale building lectures, the importance of discipline, security, etc.
   (ii) Lectures on the organisation and equipment, etc., of a Parachute Unit.
   (iii) Lectures on Airborne weapons, containers, gas, etc.
   (iv) Lectures on Airborne Operations.
   (v) Films.

As in instructional courses of all kinds, the need for physical exertion giving place to mental stimulation is encountered in all stages of parachuting. During this early or primary stage, subjects to be discussed should be of an elementary nature when dealing with parachutes and parachuting, since most of these subjects will be fully dealt with during later periods. Morale building lectures, coupled with subjects akin to the military aspects of parachuting should take precedence at this stage of training.

Physical Conditioning and Toughening Exercises

21. This portion of the training plays a major part in the training of a paratroop. The facilities available will govern the variety of exercises practicable under this heading, but nothing should be spared in the effort to make pupils fit, supple and hard.

The course should include physical training at least twice a day.

The Physical Training table, whilst still incorporating the standard principles of physical education, should include adapted exercises particularly suitable for parachuting technique. For this, some of the standard forms well known to P.T. Instructors, need to be modified. In certain exercises, the rounding of the back, the looking down at the ground, flattish-foot movements and other somewhat unconventional postures are desirable. Though they may offend the eye of the trained gymnast, they are necessary in helping to form certain kinetics whilst pupils are working in mass class formation under expert instruction.

BEAT DIVE FALL
(NOT APPROVED)

Fig. 1a.

BODY ROLL FALL
(APPROVED)

Fig. 1b.

The exercises should also aim at a general toning of the body and strengthening of the leg, arm and neck muscles; at inculcating the habit of keeping the feet and knees together, at the same time holding the weight well forward, with rounded shoulders and flattish feet; and the automatic heave of the arms for turning the upper body and the ability to fall smoothly in all directions, with the least possible hurt.

Two typical amendments of fundamental exercises are:—

(i) *The Jump Down.*—The erect carriage of the body, the landing with hands to the side, open knees and quickly arched feet in the controlled and standing position are changed. Instead the pupil stands with rounded back, arms up, with elbows to his sides, and looking down. He drops to the ground with feet and knees together on to flattish feet and with weight well forward. He does not remain standing, but falls down smoothly on thigh and hip and rounded back (see figs, 1a and 1b).

(ii) *The Forward Roll.*—The drive from the feet, the drive forward on to the hands, and the completion of the fall on rounded back are almost reversed. The fall starts from the feet after they have taken the initial shock of landing, and the body comes to ground in a smooth curve, part by part, in the line of least resistance and at speeds dependant upon the speed at which the pupil hits the ground.

22. Other physical conditioning and recreational exercises all of which are useful and will stimulate interest are as follows:—

Rope climbing

Agility

Obstacle training

Tug of war

Cliff scaling

Beam exercises

Close combat

Boxing

Leg exercises

Lifting and carrying

Medicine Ball exercises

Toggle bridging

23. Acclimatisation to heights is an important requirement for paratroops. This can be achieved by erecting a scaffold jungle or "trainasium." The pupils walk up long sloping ladders, through networks of upright scaffolding and climb about on ropes and metal poles, becoming all the time more accustomed to heights and assessing the ground from above. Failing this, practice on and judicious use of, platforms and various swings and scaffolding can achieve similar results.

24. To ensure that all trainees have reached a fair standard of fitness before passing on to the R.A.F. school, the following series of tests have to be passed:—

(i) Jump a ditch 9 ft. across.

(ii) Carry a man of about the same weight as the carrier a distance of 200 yards in 2 minutes, wearing equipment and carrying a rifle.

(iii) Jump a ditch 9 ft. across wearing equipment and carrying a rifle.

(iv) Climb a 12-ft. vertical rope, traverse a 20-ft. span of rope and descend another 12-ft. vertical rope (no equipment).

(v) Jump from a height of between 6 to 7 ft. to test landing and mobility of ankles and knees (no equipment).

(vi) Run and walk 7 miles in between 1 hour 15 minutes and 1 hour 25 minutes in Battle Order.

(vii) Perform three upward circles on beam at head height.

(viii) Sprint 100 yards in 16 seconds wearing equipment and carrying a rifle.

(ix) Complete obstacle course in Battle Order carrying a rifle.

(x) Box three rounds of 1 minute duration with an opponent of equal weight and standard.

(xi) A forced march test of 7 miles across hilly country is also carried out. Platoons double 100 yards and march 300 yards alternately. Full dress and equipment, including steel helmets, is worn. Each platoon proceeds as a single body, no member being allowed to overtake or be overtaken. The course has to be completed in not less than 1 hour 15 minutes and not more than 1 hour 25 minutes.

Practical Instruction

25. (i) *Military Training.*—It is necessary for a considerable amount of suitable military training to be included in the course. This covers drill, section and platoon formations, container and dropping zone drill, weapon training (including use of foreign weapons). Instruction in briefing should also be included.

(ii) *Air Experience.*—It is necessary that an airborne soldier should have considerable air experience and become air-minded. For this reason the site of the initial training centre should be near an aerodrome, and arrangements should be made for pupils to have flights. It may be that their jumping later will be done from a bomber, but this type of aircraft is not the most suitable for air experience. Aircraft with windows should be available, whence they can see out, and read maps and check routes and really feel airborne. If possible long trips should be made in order to detect those subject to air sickness.

(iii) *Instruction in Supply Dropping and Airborne Weapons.*—Instruction in the handling and loading of all types of container and supply dropping apparatus should be given.

Battle School

26. Experience has shown that at least one week spent in battle training is very desirable before the trainees proceed to the parachuting part of the course. A paratroop has first and foremost to be an efficient and keen soldier capable of fighting under all conditions either alone or with others. The battle school is designed to give him preliminary training in the kind of fighting he can expect to encounter. Fieldcraft, crossing obstacles, infiltration, camouflage, night operations, blitz course, assault course, are some of the subjects included in this week of strenuous training.

SYNTHETIC GROUND TRAINING

Introduction

27. The object of the synthetic apparatus is to produce as nearly as possible the conditions met with during actual parachuting. In this way the pupil is familiarised with the sensations of parachuting and is trained to carry out instinctively the correct physical motions and actions.

Although no synthetic apparatus can ever simulate real conditions, great scope does exist for devising parachuting apparatus which closely reproduces the correct physical movements and sensations. The aim should be to train under conditions slightly easier than the real ones, to avoid apparatus that involves a high injury risk and to keep the apparatus simple. Experience has shown that the most simple gadgets have proved the most useful, so long as they are used with enthusiasm and intelligence.

28. The period spent on the synthetic equipment is the most strenuous part of the course, and a danger exists of overdoing the use of this apparatus.

This may have the effect of bruising and straining the pupil's muscles with the result that his limbs become stiff instead of supple, and he is the more likely to injure himself when he jumps. With older pupils it is particularly important to introduce them to the synthetic apparatus gradually, otherwise it can do more harm than good.

A large variety of apparatus is desirable since the frequent or continuous use of one piece is apt to prove tedious both to mind and muscle.

The synthetic training is the most important period of the course from the parachuting point of view, because during this period the instructor gets to know his pupils intimately and he can make or mar them as parachutists. There is always a tendency to hasten this vitally important part of the training in order to go on to the more exciting part ahead, but this should be resisted with determination.

The Exit

29. The exit is the phase in parachuting where discipline and self-control are most necessary. A good exit is necessary in order to achieve:—

    (i) Avoidance of injury to the jumper.

    (ii) The correct functioning of the parachute.

    (iii) A short stick on the ground.

THE APERTURE EXIT

30. With the aperture exit a great deal of time has to be devoted to exit technique and team drill, since bad exits which result in twisting, somersaulting and rolling of, the man can affect the development of the parachute. The jumper must avoid hitting his pack on the aperture edge as he goes through, he must not allow his legs to get caught in the strops and he must not throw himself too far across the aperture as he jumps. Any of these may cause him to injure himself on the aperture edge and result in an uncontrolled exit. To ensure a good exit the jumper must leave from a dead central position, and he must leave with his body in a controlled and correct attitude. Finally he must move up to the aperture and project himself through it, more or less in one motion, in order to achieve a rapid stick.

[…]

THE DOOR EXIT

39. The Door Exit cannot readily be applied to the British bomber aircraft from which paratroop dropping is normally carried out. But it is the standard form of exit used in American aircraft of the Dakota or Hudson type.

The form of exit is far simpler inasmuch as the paratroop merely has to walk out of a door and each man can follow the one in front of him without any delay or hesitation such as occurs when legs have to be swung into position in a seated attitude. In consequence the stick is considerably faster than in the aperture type of exit; an average time is 0.7 second per man compared with over 1 second per man with the aperture type of exit.

The ground training for this type of exit is very simple and greatly shortens this aspect of training.

The attitude before exit is as follows. On the command "Stand to the door" the jumper stands in the doorway, left foot with toe over the edge, right foot about 10 in. to the rear, knees bent slightly, back straight but bent at the hips to an angle of about 45 degrees, head and shoulders just outside the door, head up with eyes on the horizon, and hands on outside of door at hip level, with palms facing backwards.

On the command "Go" the jumper pushes off with feet and hands, swinging his right foot forward and turning slightly to the left so that he faces the tail of the aircraft. His head is bent forward and his legs are together; his hands grip the reserve; if a reserve is not worn his hands should be by his sides at the attention position.

The Synthetic Apparatus (Door)

MOCK DOOR

40. Most of the training is done in a mock-up fuselage of the aircraft to be used. The door is open about 3 ft. above fibre or rubber mats and the pupils wear harness with dummy parachute packs and static lines.

(i) *Sequence of Training.*—The training is progressive and begins with the putting-on and inspection of equipment and is followed by individual exit training, the teaching of jump commands and finally practice in stick jumping.

When practising the exit the pupil takes up the correct position at the door and makes his exit, at the same time turning to his left, and landing on his feet on the mat. As he jumps he cries out "One thousand, two thousand, three thousand." The pupil is taught when and how to pull the reserve if a reserve is worn.

(ii) *Faults and their Correction.*—The following faults may need correction:—

(a) Static line in wrong position. This must be outside the left arm.

(b) Turning the body too far after exit. This will make the body twist or cause an unnecessarily severe opening shock.

(c) Looking down before jumping. Head must be held up with eyes on the horizon or there will be a tendency to somersault.

(d) Failure to bend head after jumping. This may cause a blow on the head from the lift webs when the parachute opens.

(e) Too great a haste in stick jumping. This may result in men being pushed beyond the door into the rear of the fuselage and upsetting the stick.

(f) Catching the pack on the edge of the door on exit. This may cause the parachute to open prematurely (American type).

MOCK TOWER

41. This structure consists of a small platform, with walls and roof, set on wooden props 35 ft. above the ground; entrance is by a ladder. On one wall is a mock-up of the door-way of the aircraft. Outside the door and above it a steel cable is fastened to a pole; the harness is attached to a pully on this cable; the cable runs downwards at such an angle that the pupil reaches the ground about 90 ft. from the base of the tower. The pupil makes a normal exit from the door wearing the harness. He has a free drop of about 10 ft. before the slack on the cable is taken up. He is then carried down on the cable to the ground.

This piece of apparatus is an excellent exit trainer. Unfortunately it cannot be used for stick exits. It is of no value as a landing trainer because the cable oscillates violently. It gives a good sensation of height and will pick out any pupils unduly sensitive to heights.

Aircraft Drill

42. The following section on aircraft drill is inserted here because the teaching of aircraft drill is to some extent bound up with the teaching of exit drill and the elements of both may be taught in the mock fuselage.

Aircraft drill is carried out in accordance with the standing orders relating to the type of aircraft used; in this matter reference should be made to A.P. 2543. Ground training, or training on synthetic apparatus is carried out by using dummy fuselages (i.e., unserviceable fuselages of actual dropping aircraft).

Before descents are actually made from aircraft, it is advisable to carry out the last few drills in the aircraft itself while stationary on the ground.

AIRCRAFT DRILL—APERTURE EXIT

43. A list of drills to be taught under this heading is as follows:—

(i) Stropping up.

(ii) Emplaning drill.

(iii) Assumption of "take-off " positions.

(iv) Assumption of "travelling positions."

(v) Assumption of "jumping positions."

(vi) Preparation of aircraft for jumping.

(vii) Emergency landing and ditching drill. Dinghy drill.

44. *Stropping Up.*—This is taught, after a general idea as to the positions taken up inside an aircraft has been gained during ground training, by seating pupils against dummy strop panels rigged in the hangar or ground training buildings. The pupil is made to strop up his neighbour and himself, and to inspect both. "Pin drill" must make the pupil adept at hooking up the "D" ring and snap hook, and locking them securely with the safety pin in the minimum of time and with accuracy. There is no time for fumbling and uncertainty in the confines of a darkened aircraft. The drill should enable the pupil to perform the operation blindfold by the time he is ready for his first descent from an aircraft.

45. *Emplaning.*—This is done in complete sections, and usually the actual aircraft on the tarmac is used.

The section forms up and is marched out to the aircraft, halted and formed up on the port side of the aircraft in two ranks facing the tail. The section is then numbered as rear rank even numbers, and front rank odd numbers; on the order "Section—right and left turn," the front rank turns to the left, the rear rank to the right; Number 9 enters the aircraft first and sits on the starboard side of the fuselage;

all the odd numbers go in first and the even numbers follow on sitting alternately. This is done so that all the odd numbers, who will eventually jump from forward of the aperture, will be in their jumping order in front of the hole, while even numbers who jump from aft of the aperture will be in their jumping order behind the aperture.

Before the section emplanes the instructor teaches the section to make a thorough inspection of their parachutes and to look for the following items:—

(a) Correct fitting of harness.

(b) Release box fastened properly.

(c) Shoulder tie and pack tie firm.

(d) Static line free and held in left hand.

The Section Leader's parachute is inspected by the last man of the section before emplaning.

Care must be taken by the instructor to see that the pupil realises his increased bulk due to his full jumping kit, and this is especially noticeable as he attempts the entry through the door of the aircraft, and also when manoeuvring inside.

46. *The Take-off and Landing Position.*—The paratroops are crowded to the front of the aircraft for take-off to distribute the weight better and enable the tail to be raised. The aperture doors are closed and the section are taught to crouch, as nearly as possible in their jumping order, as far up in the fore part of the fuselage as possible until they receive word from the pilot that the aircraft is airborne.

NOTE.—The same procedure must be adopted for a crash landing or should the flight be abandoned after take-off and the plane return with its full load of troops, to make a landing. The "take-off" positions should be taken up as the plane approaches to land.

47. *Travelling Positions.*—During actual training, this stage of the aircraft drill will not normally be used since the Dropping Ground will be within a few minutes flight of the airfield. However, "take-off" and travelling positions may be practised on the last descent (platoon in formation), if necessary.

Pupils should be shown that whenever there is an exercise or operation entailing a long flight, it is not necessary to sit rigidly in the jumping position, but that they can take up a more comfortable position in other approved parts of the aircraft.

48. *Jumping Positions.*—These are normally assumed in training directly after take-off and constitute the order of jumping from before and behind the aperture, e.g., in the Whitley the plan for the jumping positions is shown in Fig. 9.

Odd numbers in front in the order shown, even numbers are, with Number 1 at the side of the aperture and at right angles to it ready to swing his legs into the aperture on the "Action Stations" signal which is given by the RED light of the two

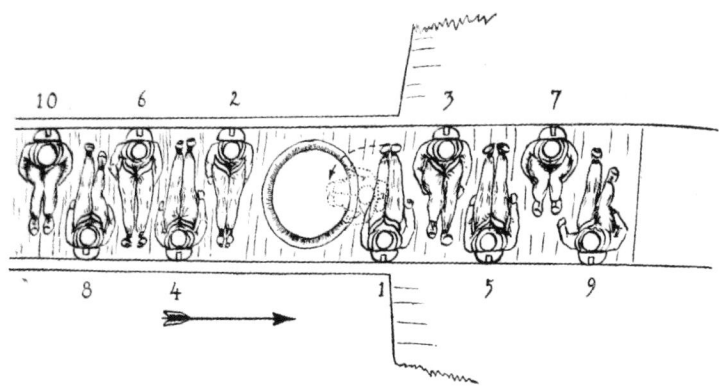

Fig. 9. Jumping positions—aperture exit.

jumping lights. On receipt of the "GO" or GREEN light, Number 1 makes his exit, followed in numerical order by the remainder of the section.

49. *Preparation of the Aircraft for Jumping.*—

This is usually practised in conjunction with the last descent. It consists of opening and fastening back the aperture cover doors when the command to prepare for jumping is given, and the stowage of the travelling mats and other movable equipment that might get caught up or interfere with the drop.

50. *Abandoning Aircraft.*—The drill for abandoning the particular aircraft in the event of emergency or forced landing must be learned, so that the correct procedure may be followed by all paratroops and an orderly and disciplined exit from the aircraft made.

All aircraft drill will necessarily vary according to the type of aircraft in use at the training school and also at the operational units. Pupils should be initiated into these variations so that they know what to expect when they proceed on their exercises at Operational Units after initial training.

AIRCRAFT DRILL—DOOR EXITS

51. *Emplaning Drill.*—The instructions in this section are based on the Dakota aircraft. The section about to emplane falls in with parachutes on, in the following order

REAR RANK: 2 4 6 8 10
FRONT RANK: 1 3 5 7 9

This is for a stick of 10 men, but any additional numbers are added in the same order of even numbers rear rank, odd numbers front rank.

The Section Commander or Instructor will then check over all the parachutes of his section as in Aircraft Drill—Aperture Exits—to ensure that each parachute is correctly fitted. He will then march the men off to the aircraft detailed.

The Section approaches the door and the N.C.O. i/c Section will, by giving the necessary words of command, form the section facing the tail of the aircraft. The plane will then be inspected for jumping, strong points, cable hooks, etc., to ensure that the plane is serviceable.

The section is then inspected by the N.C.O. to check again that the parachutes are all correctly fitted, and the section is ready to emplane.

The section then does a turn to the left and emplanes forming single file as it does so. The first man to enter is the highest number, i.e., No. 10 from the rear rank. The next in order is No. 9 from the rear rank, and so follow Nos. 8, 7, 6 and so on until they are all emplaned.

52. *Take-off and Travelling Positions.*—On entering the aircraft, even numbers will seat themselves on the right or starboard side and odd numbers on the left or port side. So that the highest number (No. 10) is in the seat furthest forward and No. 1 is nearest the door. The pilot may require the section to move along the seats as far as possible towards the front to assist in trimming the aircraft.

53. *Exit Drill.*—The procedure for door jumping with American Type Parachute is given in the American Training Manual. The paratroops remain rested until the jump-master gives the commands which precede the descent. These are the following:—

    (i) "Stand-up."—At this command the jumper stands up and faces the rear of the plane. With his right hand he breaks the static line fastener loose from the harness, where it has been held by a loop of light string. Then he takes it in his left hand keeping the static line outside the arm, and holds it in front of him, top up.

    (ii) "Hook up."—At this he grasps the anchor cable with the right hand to steady it, and with the left hand snaps the static line fastener to the cable by a sharp downward pull, which automatically locks the safety button.

    (iii) "Check Equipment."—At this command the last but one man checks the static line and equipment of the men to his front and rear; all the other men inspect the equipment of the men in front.

NOTE: Checking of Equipment.—The equipment check which is made by the instructor before emplaning and by the men themselves in the aircraft before jumping should cover the following points

American Type Parachute

    (a) Lacing of back pack must be intact.

    (b) Static line fastener properly attached to anchor cable.

(c) Static line over left arm not under.

(d) All snap hooks fastened.

(e) Rip-cord grip on reserve parachute properly housed.

British X Type Parachute

(a) Quick release box properly fastened.

(b) Shoulder straps of harness properly adjusted.

(c) Static line in proper position and not through harness.

(iv) "Call off Equipment Check."—At this the last man of the stick, e.g. No. 13 cries out "Number 13 O.K." and touches number 12 on the back. Number 12 shouts out "Number 12 O.K." and so on down the line until Number 1 cries out "All O.K."

(v) "Stand at the Door."—At this the jumper moves toward the door, sliding the static line fastener along the cable with his left hand; on reaching the door he slides the fastener to the end of the cable, checking that the static line does not fall under his arm as he takes his hand off. Then he stands in the door, left foot with toe over the edge, right foot about ten inches to the rear, knees slightly bent, back crouched to an angle of about 45 degrees, hands on outside of door at hip level, head and shoulders outside in the prop-blast, head up, eyes on the horizon.

(vi) "Go."—At this command the parachutist, without hesitation, shoves off pushing with feet and hands, swinging his right foot forward and turning slightly to the left, thus facing towards the tail. He grips the ends of the reserve in his hands, right hand on, but not clutching the rip cord handle. The head bends forward and the body is held upright with feet together. At the moment of jumping he begins counting: "One thousand, two thousand, three thousand" in a natural conversational tone. This should take about three seconds; if the opening jerk has not been felt by that time the pupil pulls the rip cord.

54. For Stick Exits, at the command "Stand up," all jumpers rise, face the door and break their snap-hook fasteners; action at the commands "Hook Up," "Check Equipment" and "Call off Equipment Check" is as before. At the command "Stand in the Door" Number 1 stands in the door as before. Number 2 stands just behind him, still holding his static line in his left hand, and places his right hand on the door just above Number One's right hand; his right foot is just beside Number One's right foot, his left foot about ten inches behind his right. When Number One has made his exit Number Two takes his left hand off his static-line and puts it on the left side of the door, at the same time sliding his right hand down slightly. He brings up his left foot to where Number One's left foot was and is ready to make his exit. Number Three stands behind Number Two with his left foot just beside Number Two's left foot, his right about ten inches to the rear. When Number Two steps into

the door-way Number Three takes a step forward with his right foot and assumes the position previously held by Number Two. The other jumpers shuffle up behind each other with the left foot forward. The drill is easier to teach if the change from the Number Three to the Number Two position is emphasised by stamping with the right foot as it is brought forward.

55. For door jumping with the X type parachute the procedure is similar. With the C-47 the static line is attached to the starboard wall of the fuselage reaching down to floor level near the door. Pupils must be careful not to become entangled in the static lines as they move down the fuselage; this is particularly liable to occur if the aircraft is taking evasive action while the men are standing up. The opening shock is negligible and there is no reserve worn. Twisting and somersaulting are rare.

56. If containers are being dropped, they are dropped either at the end of the section of ten or, more usually, since the Dakota aircraft is capable of carrying two sticks of ten (twenty men in all), they are dropped by the despatcher at the end of the first stick of ten men, and before he gives the word "Go " for the remaining stick. This is not an automatic business as in the aperture exit, when No. 5 releases the containers through pulling the container switch down by a cord attached to his static-line, but, in the case of the Dakota is done by a small bomb-firing switchboard by the side of the door of the aircraft.

The Descent

57. The descent can be considered to begin from the time that the canopy opens, and to continue until the paratroop touches the ground, a period covering some thirty to fifty seconds. Control over the parachute and the body during this descent is the vital matter which has to be taught under this heading.

To achieve adequate control the pupil is taught how to deal with the various situations which may arise during the descent; and he is also taught how to prepare himself for the landing.

58. Control in the air may be divided into three parts:—

(i) *Correction of Faults*

These usually arise from poor exits and include:—

    (a) Overcoming the effects of twisted rigging lines.

    (b) Overcoming the effects of somersaulting, i.e., extraction of limbs caught up in rigging lines.

(ii) *Flight*

During which two main items have to be considered:—

    (a) Damping of oscillation.

    (b) Holding the correct attitude.

(iii) Preparation for Landing

Which forms the major portion of the section and concerns:—

    (a) Taking up correct attitude for landing.

    (b) Emergency measures.

The tabulation of the events as enumerated above takes them in order of occurrence rather than in order of importance. The most important of the items may be considered to be turning in the air, taking up the correct attitude for landing and damping of oscillation. But as none of these can be successfully accomplished without correction of other items, it is convenient to describe the methods employed to tackle all these problems in the order indicated above.

Correction of Faults

59. (i) Twists.—In the event of the pupil encountering twists in the rigging lines after the canopy has deployed, it should be impressed upon him, that, as in other faults which may have to be overcome, there is no need for alarm, and that if he takes a calm and intelligent interest at the outset, these faults can easily be overcome.

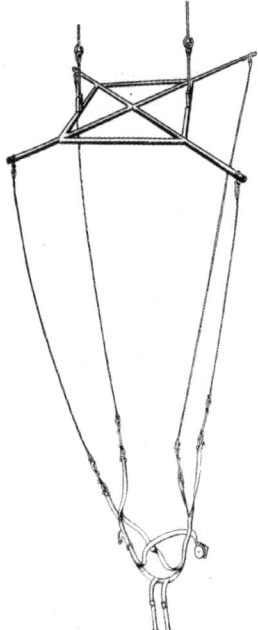

Fig. 11. Oscillation special swing.

In the case of twisted rigging lines, the pupil practises on the synthetic landing trainer apparatus without the suspension straps, attached. The pupil grasps the small lift webs attached to the metal bar, the wires supporting the apparatus having first been twisted to the right or the left. At the outset it is essential for the pupil to grasp which way the lines have been twisted, and act accordingly.

There are two methods employed for un-twisting:—

(a) The pupil takes the weight of his body on the lift webs and keeping his legs and feet together, brings a circular swinging motion of the hips and legs by circling the feet in the same direction as the twists. This is continued until the twists are free. The advantage of this method lies in the fact that at all times the pupil is in the correct position for landing, feet and knees together, knees slightly bent. But it is often found that the pupil is unable to overcome the natural tendency to circle the feet against the twist.

(b) If the required results are not obtained by method (a) then the feet may be separated, and a normal circular motion, induced against the twists with the feet kicking out, may be tried. If this method is used a careful watch must be kept on the ground, so that the feet may be brought together again as the landing becomes imminent.

Should the lines tangle as well as twist, the pupil should grasp the lift webs and jerk them violently up and down; he should not shake them sideways as this may force the twist higher up the left webs and aggravate the condition.

(ii) *Arms and Legs Caught Up in Rigging Lines.*—A further trouble, consequent upon bad exits, caused by not keeping the feet together and the arms down to the sides until the canopy develops, may be that of getting the feet or arms, or in severe cases, both, caught up in the rigging lines. Again, the pupil must be reminded that coolness and prompt action are necessary.

The pupil is suspended in the harness swing, to which cords representing the rigging lines are attached. The instructor then deliberately entangles the pupil's leg or arm in the lines and hauls them up so that the position assumed during entanglement is simulated. The pupil is then instructed to lever off the lines that are round his leg by bringing up the other foot and pushing them down the leg, assisting with his hands. If his arms are entangled, these should be freed first. At the same time this serves to demonstrate to the pupil that he can let go of his lift webs with his hands and still be held securely in the parachute harness. All this helps to give confidence against the rather strong fear which certain pupils occasionally acquire after discussing such an eventuality.

Flight Control

60. (i) *Damping Oscillation: Description of Apparatus.*—This is taught on a special swing (see fig. 11) which consists of a wide framework (A), attached at two points (B, B) to the roof.

From each corner of the framework is suspended a cable, two of these being in front and two behind, representing the four groups of rigging lines of the parachute. To the lower end of these cables is attached the normal parachute harness on short strips of elastic cords to give a certain pliancy, and the pupil sits in the harness. The whole apparatus is pivoted at the points (B, B) and swings backwards and forwards in a wide arc to simulate forward and backward oscillation. Sideways oscillations may also be set up by inducing a side swing on the apparatus by pushing in that direction.

(ii) *Damping Oscillation—Operation of Apparatus*—The drawback of this apparatus is that, whilst the mechanical action of damping can be taught, this action does not reduce the pendulum motion as rapidly as might be expected owing to the top of the apparatus being anchored and not mobile as with an airborne canopy.

As the pupil sits swinging backwards and forwards, he is taught to watch his canopy, to change his grip from front to back lift webs, and to be free and comfortable in his movements. Then for damping oscillation he is taught to grasp the forward lift webs and pull as the forward edge of the canopy begins to rise, and to maintain a strong steady pull until the highest point is reached and then gently to relax his pull. This movement is repeated on each forward swing. Later, if the Instructor feels his pupil to be capable, he may teach him to do the similar movement on the back lift webs during the backward swing, but he must be careful not to confuse the issue and, by bad timing, increase the oscillation instead of lessening it.

A sideways oscillation is treated in similar manner, only that the pull against the direction of the swing is made by grasping both lift webs together on the side on which the canopy is rising.

61. Other methods of damping oscillation have been found to be useful, and are mentioned for information and consideration. They should only be used in practise if the pupil feels himself to be master of the situation.

Oscillation is "rhythmic swinging." Disturbance of this rhythm will reduce the swinging; the methods mentioned below all have this disturbance of the rhythm as their object.

(i) *Quick Turns.*—One or more quick turns, by jerk of the redistribution of weight, reduce and sometimes completely damp oscillation, but quick action is needed, and when near the ground, the novice may induce an incorrect landing position from the last turn that he has made.

(ii) *See-sawing.*—By rapid and strong see-sawing of the lift webs from side to side, forward and backward oscillation may be damped, and lateral oscillation reduced if timed correctly. If this is carried out too near the ground, the pupil is in danger of leaving his landing assessment until too late, and also, if the timing is inaccurate, the oscillation can be increased.

(iii) *Turning Across.*—Finally, in cases of mild, or gentle oscillation, the remedy is simply to turn across the oscillation, thus transforming the fore and aft oscillation into a mild sideways one. Directly side-ways landings can be effected with ease and safety with only a mild oscillation in this direction.

(iv) *Altering the shape of the Parachute.*—Another method of damping oscillation which has proved very effective, is to reach up as high as possible on the two front lift webs, pull them downwards and hold them there: this produces a partial collapse of the periphery of the parachute on one side; there is a slightly increased rate of descent, but oscillation is noticeably reduced. If this position is held until the parachutist reaches the ground, certain modifications in landing technique are necessary. The adoption of this method of reducing oscillation is under consideration.

62. *Holding Correct Attitude.*—The vital importance of this must be driven home from the moment the pupil is introduced to the apparatus connected with, or used for, flight control. When on the Harness Swing practising turns, or on the Winch practising falls, or whatever the apparatus may be, the correct attitude must be demonstrated to the pupil and he must be constantly reminded of it during the performance of his other exercises. The reason for this is that a good landing is dependent on the correct body attitude being adopted prior to touching the ground. To ensure that this will always be the case the assumption of the correct attitude should become an instinctive and automatic action throughout the descent. The legs should be together, knees and ankles firm, soles of the feet flush and in the same plane, legs slightly bent with the angle of the ankles adjustable during the swing, so that the soles of the feet will always be parallel with the ground surface, and the legs, though pressed firmly together, not so tense as to resist contact with the ground.

During the swing, the pupil must maintain his centre of gravity as nearly as possible as if he were standing with knees semi-flexed, in a leaning forward position. To do this, he must press his body forward on the forward swing, and backward on the backward swing. Finally, the pupil must reach well up on the lift webs with his hands.

63. *Preparation for Landing.*—Turning, in order to face the line of drift, and so effect a forward landing, is the most important part of flight control and requires most time for teaching. Since the paratroop must avoid landing backwards, it is essential to be able rapidly and instinctively to turn himself in the air so that he comes down facing forwards.

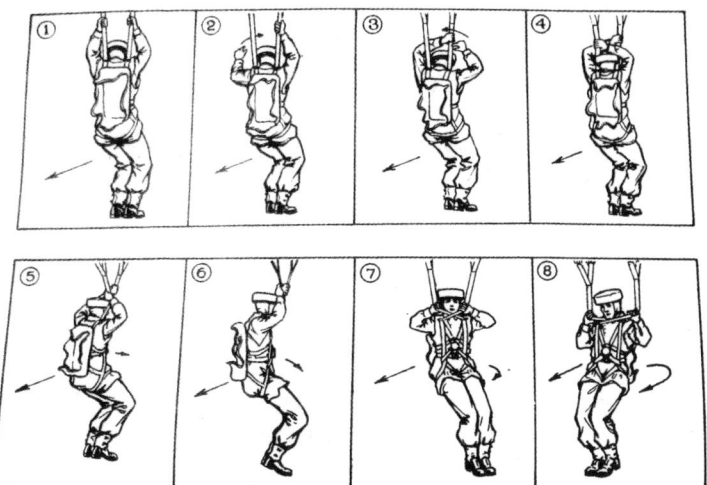

Fig. 14. Phases of the turn.

If during the descent, the ground, trees, or any objects seem to be going away from him, then he is travelling in a backwards direction, and will fall backwards on landing unless he makes a turn. When assessing direction of drift, anywhere in the forward or obliquely forward field of view may be considered as forward; but the pupil must not look backwards over his shoulder to assess his direction because this produces a very bad body position with a straight back. If any part of the full forwards field is not coming towards him then he must turn.

CHAPTER 2
AIRBORNE EQUIPMENT

As discussed in the introduction to this book, paratroopers largely went into action with only the weapons and equipment that they could carry personally, or which could be dropped in special containers. For weaponry, about their person they would usually have a rifle, submachine gun or carbine, pistol and a handful of grenades; the drop containers would include light and medium machine guns, light mortars, specialist demolition charges, man-portable anti-tank weapons and also elements such as rations and other important supplies to extend the duration of the operation. Even heavier equipment could be deployed either on gliders or as special palletised loads. Of course, the paratrooper would also be carrying his parachute equipment, either a main chute and reserve chute or just (as in the case of British airborne forces) a main chute. All told, the soldier would be at the limit of his physical carrying capability – the average paratrooper might be carrying between 90 and 120lb (40–55kg) of equipment, including the parachute. In the US Army's FM 31-30, *Tactics and Techniques of Airborne Troops* (1942), we see a breakdown of the typical equipment, plus some of the heavier materiel taken into action.

From FM 31-30, *Tactics and Techniques of Airborne Troops* **(1942)**

45. Equipment.—*a*. See Table of Basic Allowances No. 7.

b. Equipment carried by the individual parachutist is shown in figures 2 and 3. This may be varied, depending upon the situation and the mission of the unit. Items that may be carried, in addition to those shown, include demolition equipment, signal equipment, bayonet, extra ammunition, medical equipment, and the carbine. The amount of equipment carried is limited to that which allows a safe rate of descent. The type of equipment is limited by the fact that any protruding angular objects may foul the suspension lines of the canopy, and the possibility that such objects may cause serious injury to the parachutist, who may have to roll or tumble upon landing.

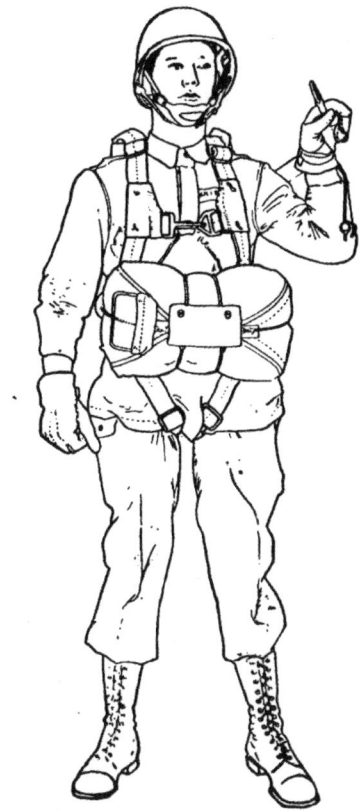

Fig. 2. Individual parachutist wearing T-5 troop type parachute and complete jumping equipment.

	Pounds
Helmet, steel, with liner	2.7
Parachute assembly, type T-5, complete (main pack on back, reserve pack on chest, static line, and static snap with safety pin)	33.5
Watch, wrist, 7-jewel	0.053
Ration (carried in pants leg)	0.75
Clothing worn:	
Suit, parachutist, jumping, summer (two piece)	3.7
Boots, parachutist	4.4
Gloves, horsehide, unlined	0.282
Undershirt, cotton; drawers, cotton; socks, light wool; and identification tags	0.625
Articles carried in pockets:	
Center chest pocket:	
Knife, pocket, M-2, with thong	0.3
Right chest pocket:	
Maps, message book, and pencil	0.344
Left chest pocket:	
Toilet tissue	0.125
Compass, watch	0.125
Whistle (when needed)	0.125
Right waist pocket:	
Grenade, hand, fragmentation	1.25
Left waist pocket:	
Grenade, hand, fragmentation	1.25
Right leg pocket:	
Pistol, automatic, caliber .45 loaded with a clip of 7 rounds	2.762
Two extra clips, each loaded with 7 rounds	0.962
Handkerchief	0.053
Left leg pocket:	
Rope, parachutist, 20-foot length	1.0
Packet, first-aid	0.234

Fig. 3. Side view of individual parachutist, showing main canopy, pack on back, and reserve parachute on chest.

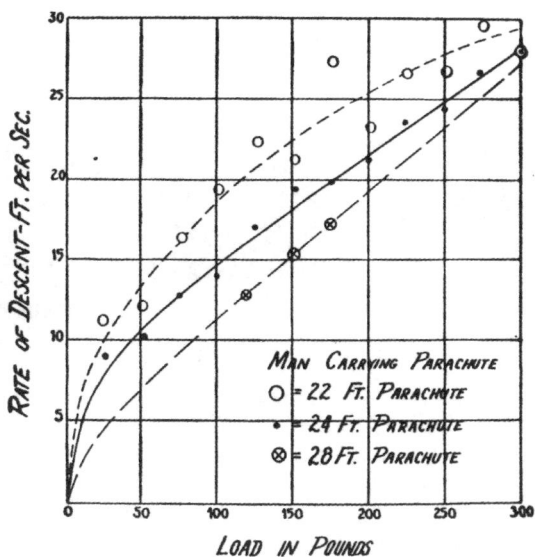

Fig. 4. Graph showing performance of various sizes of canopies.

[. . .]

46. Delivery Units—*a. Definition.*—delivery unit is a parachute device used for transporting equipment or supplies from an airplane in flight to the ground. It consists of three main parts: the container or harness, the canopy, and the pack assembly.

b. Types.—There are three general types of delivery units, classified according to loads carried:

(1) *Unit type.*—Those designed to carry squad or unit loads of arms and equipment for initial entry into combat.

(2) *General types.*—Those designed to carry food, water, gas masks, medical supplies, certain types of ammunition, and other miscellaneous equipment or supplies.

(3) *Special types.*—Those designed to carry one particular piece of equipment or item of supply, such as boxed ammunition, carts, motorcycles, or crates containing pigeons.

c. Unit type, A-5.—(1) THE delivery unit, type A-5, consists of a roll type container, a 24-foot circular cotton canopy, and a conventional "pull off" pack assembly. (See fig. 5.)

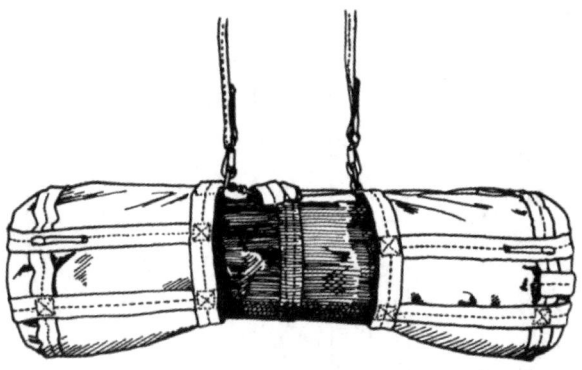

Fig. 5. Type A-5 aerial delivery unit.

(2) The container consists of three parts: 1 felt-padded center section of 22 oz. duck, 56 inches by 180 inches, in which arms and equipment are placed and rolled into a bundle 44 inches long and 18 inches in diameter; and 2 end caps, which fit over the ends of the rolled center section and fasten together by 2 male and female harness fasteners on opposite sides of the roll. The end caps are equipped with 2 V-rings for attaching the risers of the canopy, and 2 V-rings for suspending the unit on bomb racks.

(3) The canopy has 2 risers, connected by a bridle just below the suspension lines, by means of which the container is suspended during descent. These are attached to the suspension lines at one end, and by means of snap fasteners to the V-rings on the container at the other.

(4) The pack assembly consists of a circular pack tray and pack cover into which the canopy is packed in the conventional manner. The pack is attached to one end of the container by tie strings and is opened by means of a 15-foot static line.

d. General types.—(1) *Type A-4.*—*(a)* The delivery unit, type A-4, container consists of a box-type container, a 24-foot circular cotton canopy, and a conventional "pull off" pack assembly. (See fig. 6.)

Fig. 6. Type A-4 aerial delivery unit.

(b) The container is a rectangular bag of duck, 30 by 24 by 12 inches, reinforced on the bottom by plywood, and on top by a metal frame which includes rings for suspension on bomb racks. It has a suitable suspension harness of webbing. Inside the bag may be placed 2 cardboard or light wooden boxes, each 12 by 12 by 30 inches. However, supplies may be packed in the bag without the use of boxes.

(c) The canopy and pack are of the types used with the delivery unit, type A-5.

(2) *Type A–6.*—*(a)* The delivery unit, type A-6, consists of a box type container, a 24-foot circular cotton canopy, and a conventional "pull off" pack assembly. (See fig. 7.)

Fig. 7. Type A-6 aerial delivery unit.

(b) The container consists of two parts: a rectangular duck bag with a suitable suspension harness of webbing; and an inner, replaceable, commercial corrugated fiber box, 12 by 12 by 30 inches.

(c) The canopy and pack are of the types used with the delivery unit, type A-5.

e. Special type A-7.—(1) The delivery unit, type A-7, consists of a harness sling, a 24-foot circular cotton canopy and a conventional "pull off" pack assembly. (See fig. 8.)

Fig. 8. Type A-7 ammunition delivery unit with canopy in pack preparatory to dropping.

(2) The harness is constructed of cotton webbing to fit boxed small-arms ammunition and 37-mm ammunition. It has 2 V-rings for attaching the risers of the canopy.

(3) The canopy and pack are of the types used with the delivery unit, type A-5.

f. Loadings of unit type.—Loads for the delivery unit, type A-5, are limited to 200 pounds, including the weight of the containers.

g. Loadings of general types.—(1) Loads for delivery units, types A-4 and A-6, are limited to 200 pounds, including the weight of the containers.

(2) Care must be taken that there are no sharp edges or protruding surfaces upon which the total shock of landing might fall. Brittle or breakable items must be well protected by padding.

h. Loadings of the special types.—Since special type delivery units are developed for particular items of equipment, each is constructed to accommodate the load desired. In general, the size of canopy depends upon the weight of the items to be dropped. The following precautions should be observed:

(1) *Delivery unit, type A-7.*—Remove wing bolts and open tin liner prior to placing in harness.

(2) *Packing 81-mm mortar.*—The 81-mm mortar can be readily packed In the standard type A-5 delivery unit in the following manner:

    (a) Adjust the bipod so that a block of wood, 5 by 5 inches can be placed between the ends of the legs, and place the elevation and traverse vernier to face the center of the roll when packed.

    (b) Wrap the sight in ¾-inch felt padding, place between the legs of the bipod, and wrap the chain around all three to prevent shifting. (See figs. 9 and 10.)

Fig. 9. Type A-5 aerial delivery container, showing base plate rig for dropping 81-mm mortar complete. The barrel and bipod are inside the roll.

Fig. 10. 81-mm mortar displayed after being dropped in an A-5 aerial delivery unit.

(c) Stow the base plate outside the roll with its ends entering the end caps of the container. Two additional pieces of "1200 lbs." webbing are necessary to hold the base plate in place and prevent shifting. The arrangement of the additional webbing is shown in figure 9. The base plate is stowed opposite the points of suspension so that it will land at the bottom of the roll.

(3) *Other special loadings.*—For dropping guns, small vehicles, and other special loads, there are available 48-foot and 36-foot heavy duty canopies. These large canopies, as well as clusters of smaller standard canopies, may be used for heavy loads. See figures 11 and 12 for the performance of these canopies in carrying various loads.

The US Military Intelligence Service produced analytical reports on all the enemy combatants, assessing the strengths and weaknesses of their operational capability. By 1942, the German airborne forces were a natural source of interest, especially as US airborne forces were in development at this time. Here the report *Enemy Air-Borne Forces* focuses on equipment and uniform. Note the information about the stimulants taken by the paras in operations. 'Pervitin' is actually a methamphetamine, and was used heavily by German forces throughout the war – 35 million tablets alone were ordered for military use just prior to the invasion of France in 1940. The drug produces feelings of euphoria, wakefulness and courage, and its contributory effect to the outcome of airborne missions can only be guessed at.

From *Enemy Air-Borne Forces* (1942)

19. UNIFORM AND EQUIPMENT OF GERMAN PARACHUTE TROOPS

The parachute rifleman, as a member of the German Air Force possesses an ordinary German Air Force uniform. This uniform has yellow collar patches (except possibly in the case of some specialists) and the name of the regiment embroidered on the cuff, but this is taken off before the soldier leaves the home station of the regiment. In action only the jacket of this uniform is worn, though the garrison (overseas) cap is also taken. The remainder of the combat uniform is peculiar to parachute troops.

a. Trousers

These are like skiing trousers, quite long and loose, and gray in color. They have buttoned pockets on the sides of the thighs in which such articles as garrison (overseas) caps and swastika flags are kept.

b. Helmet

This is round in shape, and is thickly padded with rubber, with a narrow brim and practically no neck-shield. It is varnished a matt blue-gray, or mottled, color, and bears ordinary German Air Force insignia. The strap forks below the ear, and is attached to the helmet at four points. The helmet is commonly worn with a cloth cover, frequently with a light-colored cross on top (the purpose of which is unknown) and with a band round it for insertion of camouflage; the band may be colored for purposes of recognition.

c. Coveralls

This garment is of waterproof gabardine, loose fitting and fastened by a zipper fastener up the front. The color is normally olive green (or gray-green), now usually mottled. The legs are cut short some distance above the knee; the sleeves are long and button at the wrist. On both sleeves are worn large-size "wings" as stripes of rank; on the right breast is the German Air Force flying eagle (*Hoheitszeichen*). There are two very capacious pockets on the thighs, two more on the chest, and slits at each hip; pockets are closed by zipper fasteners. The coveralls are worn over uniform and equipment for the jump; on landing, the garment is taken off and usually put on again under the equipment.

d. Gloves

These are of padded leather, with long gauntlets which grip by means of elastic; sometimes woolen gloves are substituted. They are worn only for the jump.

e. Boots

These are of heavy leather, and have thick rubber soles with a V-pattern tread. They are laced up the side, and there is a seam up the front. They extend some way above the ankle, and the trousers are tucked into them; the tops fit tightly.

f. Knee Protectors

These are of rubber, in thick horizontal bars, rather like those which some U.S. basketball players wear. They are strapped on over the trouser knee, and are discarded after the jump.

g. Ankle Bandages

These are of linen, and are bound around instep and ankle, and about one-third of the way up the leg. The heel is left free, and the bandages are not removed after the jump.

h. Gas Mask

Of normal type, this is carried in a special canvas container. The new gas mask (*Gasmaske 40*) is made of pure and very strong rubber. An antigas cape of oilcloth is also taken.

i. Identifications

The parachutist's badge, worn low on the left breast, is a diving eagle, golden-colored, in a wreath of oak and bay of oxidized silver color; the eagle holds a swastika in its claws. (The German Army parachutist's badge is slightly different.) This badge is not worn except at home stations. An identity disc is carried; but pay-books (*Soldbücher*) are handed in on leaving home stations, and a camouflaged identity card (*Tarnausweis* or *Feindflugausweis*) is taken instead.

j. Parachutes

Types RZ16, RZ1, or 36DS28 are known. Type RZ16—*Rückenfallschirm Zwangsauslösung* 16 (back-pack, compulsion-opening parachute, type 16)—since the beginning of 1941 has been replacing the RZ1, which opens sometimes with a dangerous jerk. The RZ16, because of its ingenious construction, opens without shock, and its opening is said to be 100 percent sure. The parachutes used in jumping schools are pure silk and are valued at 1,000 marks apiece; but the combat parachutes, intended for use only once, are made of artificial silk, or "macoo." The suspension lines are drawn together a few feet above the belt of the parachutist's harness, to the back of which they are attached by two hemp harness cords; in the air, the man seems to dangle from a single string. With the airplane traveling at 80 to 100 miles per hour, the standard height of drop is just under 400 feet. After a clear drop of about 80 feet, the parachute takes over and the subsequent rate of descent is 16 to 17 feet per second (11 miles per hour). Reports on colored parachutes are various—black, white or beige, brown, and green are all used; the principal purpose seems to be ease of recognition, though there may be some small camouflage effect against the ground (but not against the sky).

k. Individual Weapons

The combat pistol (*Kampfpistole*) is a kind of 25-mm (about 1-inch caliber) Very pistol (*Leuchtspistole*), but the barrel is rifled. Besides a signal cartridge, a special cartridge can be fired containing as projectile a light metal cylinder filled with scrap iron mixed with an inflammable, corrosive substance. The weapon has a strong recoil, and for that reason must be fired with both hands. The best range is about 55 yards, and bursts from the exploding projectile cover a radius of about 20 yards.

The automatic pistol 40 [MP40] is a 35-caliber (9-mm) weapon with a length of about 20 inches. The sights, fixed at 110 yards, are adjustable to twice that distance. The 32-cartridge magazine functions poorly if filled with more than 24 cartridges. A good marksman can effectively fire in practice only about 4 charges of 24 cartridges per minute, though the pistol is said to have a decidedly higher rate of theoretical fire.

For the jump, the parachutist formerly carried only a large jackknife and an automatic pistol (*Pistole 08*) with two magazines. Men in the first platoons to land, however, might carry up to four hand grenades, and about one man in four of them a machine carbine. Since the end of March 1942, German parachutists have been required to jump with this latter weapon. Other weapons come down in weapon containers attached to "load parachutes." Experiments are being encouraged in which the individual is dropped with what he is normally equipped when operating in his combat section.

l. Rations

Rations taken, including those in the arms containers, may last German parachutists for 2 or even 3 days. Further supplies are dropped in "provisions bombs," which are described below. Special foods taken include Wittler bread, sliced and wrapped, which is supposed to last indefinitely until unwrapped (but, in fact, does not); chocolate mixed with kola (*Schokokola*), and with caffeine (*Kobona*), which is not believed to be any better than ordinary chocolate; and simple refreshing foods like grape sugar. Most of the food is quite ordinary.

m. Drugs and First-Aid Supplies

Parachute troops are not doped. But the following "drugs" are used: (1) energen or dextro-energen, in white tablets, a dextrose or glucose preparation, to produce energy; (2) pervitin, a drug allied to benzedrine, to produce wakefulness and alertness. Pervitin is said to create thirstiness.

The parachutist usually carries one large and two small field dressings. Each platoon has a noncommissioned officer as its medical aid man. The first-aid kit, with which he probably jumps, contains bandages, dressings, adhesive tape, safety pins, soap, ointments, iodine, antiseptics, and analgesics. Containers dropped by separate parachute have sometimes been found to hold small suitcases of extra medical supplies and surgical instruments. Each combat company has a stretcher. Since the rate of casualties may be high, the XIth Air-Borne Corps has four medical companies, one of which is probably an air-landing field hospital company. Ju-52s, which will carry eight lying casualties, may be utilized to evacuate the severely wounded to Germany.

n. Arms Containers

Such equipment as the parachutists do not carry in the jump may be dropped in containers. Four standard arms containers are carried in each Ju-52. Each container weighs 50 to 60 pounds empty and takes a load of up to 260 pounds. Three different models have been identified: (1) a cylindrical container 5 feet long and 16 to 18 inches in diameter, hinged along its length so that it can be opened in half; (2) a container of the same length but of square cross-section, 16 inches by 16 inches, with beveled edges and hinged along its length so that one long side opens as a lid; (3) a container similar to the preceding but hinged along one long edge so that it opens in half like a trombone case. This is probably an improved design. All three of these containers are dropped in a similar manner. They are painted in various bright colors, with rings and other markings denoting the unit for which intended. Some containers have been described as fibre trunks 6 by 1½ by 1½ feet.

o. Contents of Arms Containers

Heavy mortars, weighing 125 pounds, and other equipment of the heavy weapons company would undoubtedly go into arms containers. Explosives of all kinds are taken, including AT and antipersonnel mines. Radio equipment goes into containers that are specially padded. Among miscellaneous articles that have been dropped by the container method have been antigas protective clothing, and particularly tools and spare parts, such as spark plugs, useful in operating commandeered motor vehicles.

p. "Provisions Bombs" (Versorgungsbomben)

These are carried in bomb racks and released like ordinary bombs, which they resemble in shape. Any bomber aircraft may be expected to drop them on positions where troops have been landed some time previously. The "bomb" is about 6 feet in length and 1½ feet in diameter, having a separate compartment at the end to contain the parachute. On release of the "bomb," this end cap is torn off and the parachute is pulled out. There is no shock absorber. On suitable ground and from a low altitude, "provisions bombs" may be dropped without parachutes. Even ordinary sacks of provisions are so dropped.

q. Heavy Equipment Dropped by Parachute

Much heavy parachute-borne equipment may be thrown out the door of the Ju-52, with or without a special container. Bicycles, stretchers, small flame-throwers, mines, large mortars, light artillery pieces, and perhaps motorcycles may be dropped. The 28/20-mm AT gun, model 41, has been dropped complete and ready for action, on wheels, in a container. There is no reason why a number of other weapons could not similarly be dropped complete. In most cases they are suitable for separation into several loads, but vital time may be saved by dropping them complete. The use of several parachutes together, common in the past, has sometimes proved unsatisfactory; large parachutes are therefore being made which will take loads up to 500 pounds.

The following material from the *Parachute Training Manual* explains in some detail the types of parachute equipment used by British, American and German paratroopers. This was no mere academic matter, as the characteristics of parachute design could have a profound effect of both the paratrooper's landing – and therefore the chances of his sustaining injuries – and of his directional control in the air. The most unsatisfactory of the designs was the German RZ 1 and RZ 16, which did not have lift webs ('risers'); this meant that once the parachute had opened, the paratrooper had almost no control over the direction of descent. The design also necessitated an awkward exit procedure from the aircraft; the *Fallschirmjäger* would literally have to dive from the door head-first, and in a spread-eagled fashion, this necessary to cope with the shock of the static line deploying the parachutes. Thankfully for the Allies, parachute design was far more intelligent and controllable, and the benefits of including the lift webs are clearly outlined here.

From *Parachute Training Manual* (1942)

3. TYPES OF HARNESS AND SUSPENSION

Introduction

Fig. 41. British paratroop harness.

6. The types of harness and lift webs used with military parachutes vary in detail but are in most cases similar in principle. Four types of harness are shown in figs. 41, 42, 43 and 44 as follows:—

(i) British paratroop.

(ii) British pilot.

(iii) American paratroop.

(iv) German paratroop.

7. The fundamental requirements of a harness are that it shall:—

(a) Take the weight of the wearer when suspended in the air.

(b) Hold the wearer's body securely in the suspension position.

The former requirement is usually achieved by making the wearer sit in a sling formed by the main suspension straps which pass in a continuous line from one set of rigging lines, under the man's legs and up to the other set of rigging lines. The latter requirement is met by shoulder, back, chest, and leg straps, which hold the wearer firmly in the sling.

The part of the harness or sling above the wearer's shoulders is known as the lift-webs. The lift webs act as the junction between the body harness and the rigging lines of the parachute. Their design should enable the paratroop to exercise some control over his parachute during the descent, and they should prevent the paratroop's body fouling the rigging lines or the canopy during deployment.

8. The general design requirements therefore, of the harness and lift webs can be described as follows:—

(a) To prevent shock and injury to the paratroop on opening of the canopy.

(b) To provide a comfortable suspension position during the descent,

(c) To provide a satisfactory attitude of the body for landing shock.

(d) To permit directional control in the air during the descent.

(e) To permit a rapid release both during the descent and after landing.

(f) To assist in the carrying of equipment.

(g) To be strong and robust for frequent service use.

British Paratroop

9. The British paratroop harness is specially designed for the X type parachute and differs in some respects from the normal R.A.F. pilot type harness. The illustration at fig. 41 shows that the main suspension strap (E) is a continuous strap which passes down and just in front of the wearer's shoulders before passing under the seat. This provides the natural position in which a man would sit in a sling, i.e., with his centre of gravity over the seat strap or sling. The leg straps (D) pass round and behind the suspension strap below the back strap. This makes a very firm fit round the thigh and holds the upper part of the thigh into the seat strap. The leg strap after passing round the suspension strap is attached to one of the lower points of the quick-release box. When the release mechanism is operated the leg straps do not, fall away from the man because no suspension strain is taken on these straps or on the release box. The wearer, therefore, is still held in the harness until he has had time to disengage the straps with his hands.

The British harness is good for absorbing opening shock and provides a safe and comfortable sitting position during the descent. The position of the main suspension straps and lift webs in front of the shoulders enables the wearer to cross his lift webs during the descent without difficulty when he wishes to alter the direction in which he is facing. Owing to the position of the suspension strap under the seat, the legs are thrown slightly forward as though the wearer is sitting in a comfortable chair. This may result in a tendency to land on the buttocks and back in calm conditions, but is advantageous for a forward landing in high wind conditions.

The tight fitting of the leg straps which, prevents rapid disengagement from the harness may be disadvantageous when landing in water or when landing in high wind. A modified form of quick release is under consideration to overcome this problem.

The divided lift webs enable the paratroop to damp oscillation. On the other hand, they allow the paratroop to somersault between the division of the lift webs. It will be noticed that the lift webs do not divide until a few inches above the shoulders. Greater control over oscillation could be obtained by starting the division at the shoulders as is done in the American and pilot type harnesses.

10. The British paratroop harness is apt to give the wearer such a safe and comfortable feeling that he feels "naked" in other types of harness. This feeling is not surprising bearing in mind that the British paratroop harness absorbs approximately 24 ft. of webbing in its fully extended condition, compared with approximately 17 ft for the American and German types.

British Pilot

Fig. 42. British—Pilot Type—Parachute harness.

11. The illustration at fig. 42 shows that the main suspension strap divides and passes behind and in front of the wearer's shoulders. The rear straps cross each other on the wearer's back, whilst the front straps pass downwards through the release box. This provides a comfortable position in the air, but the legs hang more in a downwards direction than in the case of the British paratroop harness.

The leg strap passes round the front suspension strap above the waist strap. This makes the fit of the harness round the thigh looser than in the case of the British paratroop harness. There is a tendency for the wearer's weight to be taken more on the leg straps than on the seat strap unless the harness is carefully adjusted.

It is the lower part of the front suspension straps winch are attached to the lower points of the release box, and not the leg straps as with the British paratroop harness. The result of this is that when the release mechanism is operated the weight on the suspension strap causes it to fall away immediately from the wearer and he falls out of the harness. Thus it is dangerous to operate the release box of the pilot type harness whilst in the air.

The R.A.F. pilot type harness is satisfactory for absorbing opening shock. Owing to the man's body and legs being suspended more or less in a vertical position, there is less tendency to fall backwards on landing in conditions of no wind. The vertical attitude is Satisfactory for landing in light wind conditions, out is unsatisfactory for high winds.

The pilot type harness requires tighter and more careful adjustment than that of the British paratroop harness. This follows naturally from the fact that Considerably less webbing is used.

American Paratroop

12. The illustration at fig. 43 shows that the American paratroop harness is a combination of the British paratroop and pilot type. The main suspension strap passes down in front of the shoulder and round the seat, but more strain is taken on the leg straps than with the British paratroop harness. This tends to keep the legs apart. Hooks are used for connecting the harness instead of a release box (for a fuller description, see para. 37).

During the descent the man's body is in a more or less upright position similar to the R.A.F. pilot type attitude. The lift webs divide at the shoulder as in the pilot type harness.

The reserve parachute carried in front has a 22 ft. canopy, and is attached by two Snap hooks to D-rings on the main suspension straps, and secured by a broad webbing strap encircling the paratroop's body.

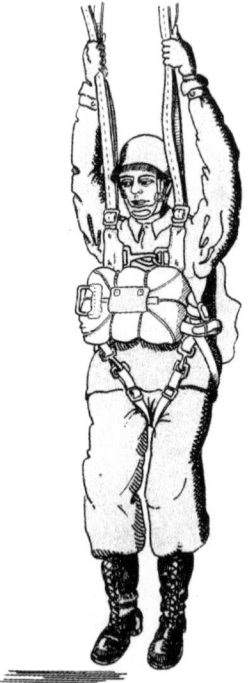

Fig. 43. American parachute harness.

To release himself from the harness the paratroop must undo the chest hook and two leg hooks; he must then undo the webbing strap holding the reserve, and unfasten one of the snap hooks by which the reserve is attached to the harness.

The American harness is not so comfortable as the British harness. Owing to the opening shock that results from the American method of canopy first deployment, it is necessary to have the harness tightly adjusted, and this causes considerable discomfort if the Wearer is obliged to wear the harness for any length of time.

In order to prevent the lift webs striking the head or face on the opening shock, it is necessary for the shoulder buckles to be adjusted as far back on the shoulders as possible. As a result of this, when the parachutist wishes to make a body turn, he is obliged to cross the lift webs behind his head; this position is more difficult to hold than the turn with the X type harness (in front of the face).

German Paratroop

13. The illustration at fig. 44 shows that the German paratroop harness is altogether lighter and simpler, and differs in design and conception from the British and American harnesses. The main suspension and leg straps are similar in design to the American harness, but the actual suspension instead of being taken on these straps from the shoulder, is taken largely on a special waist strap. The lift webs are taken from this waist strap to a single point at the end of the rigging lines. The harness is very simple as is shown by the small amount of webbing used.

Fig. 44. German parachute harness.

The method of suspension and the lack of lift webs above the wearer's head, results in the body being inclined forward during the descent. This tends to make the paratroop land in a forward position, sometimes on his hands and arms, which is satisfactory for normal wind conditions, but can be dangerous in high winds.

The lack of lift webs means that the paratroop must kick himself round if he wishes to change his direction during the descent.

To release himself the man has to undo the two hooks which hold the leg straps, and the buckle holding the waist strap.

The German harness has recently been modified by the introduction of five simple quick-release devices; these are situated as follows: one on the waist strap, one on each shoulder strap, and one on each leg strap, where they replace the snap hooks.

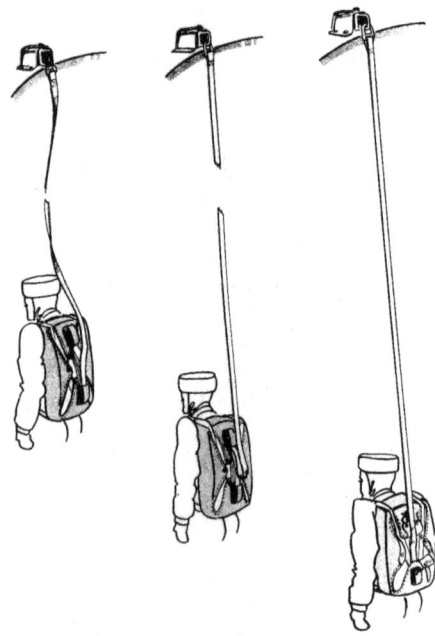

Fig. 46. Automatic operation of parachute. (Shows static line being withdrawn from pack by weight of parachutist. The lower end of the static line is tied to the apex of the canopy)

TYPES OF MILITARY PARACHUTE AND METHODS OF EXIT

14. There are various types of parachute available for military purposes. In general, it may be stated that these parachutes differ from one another in two main principles—firstly, in method of operating, and secondly, in sequence of development.

Method of Operation

15. There are two different methods of operation of parachutes:—

(i) Manual operation by the paratroop himself.

(ii) Automatic operation by a static line attached to the aircraft.

16. *Manual Operation.*—With this type the wearer jumps and falls freely through the air. He then himself pulls a cord which causes the pack to spring open and usually a small pilot parachute to be released. This pilot parachute, which is attached to the apex of the main parachute, fills with air and draws the main one out of the pack. The main parachute then fills with air and as it does so it pulls the rigging lines out of the pack and the canopy is free to develop fully. This is the method of operation usually employed for emergency parachutes.

The advantages of manual operation for the emergency parachute are set out fully in the introduction to A.P. 1182. For a military parachute it is possible to use one which is manually operated, and this has been the practice in Russia, but it means that the paratroops must be dropped from a greater height, and unless delayed opening is practicable, their vulnerability during a long descent is dangerous as is also the tendency for them to be scattered over a large area.

17. *Automatic Operation.*—With this type the opening is not controlled, in any way by the wearer. One end of a line or cord, known as the "static line," is tied to the apex of the canopy or to a pack containing the canopy. The other end of the static line is attached to a fixed point, known as the "strong point," in the aircraft. When the wearer jumps and the static line becomes taut, it either pulls the apex of the canopy out of the pack or pulls the pack away from the canopy. The wearer therefore has to do nothing himself except jump from the aircraft and wait for the parachute to develop automatically.

All military parachutes are believed to be operated on the static line principle, except in Russia.

The advantages of automatic operation of military parachutes are considerable. It ensures rapid and regular opening of all parachutes at a predetermined distance below the aircraft; this enables paratroops to be dropped with safety from a low height and results in their reaching the ground more or less at the same time. These advantages outweigh the few disadvantages which are the necessity for strong-point modifications to the aircraft, a means of withdrawing the static lines and slightly slower jumping in sticks owing to static line interference.

Sequence of Development

18. There are two methods of deployment of parachutes which are known shortly as—

(i) "Canopy first"

(ii) "Canopy last"

[. . .] The U.S.A. T-5 (training) type parachute, employed by airborne troops, is used to illustrate "canopy first" type and the British military parachute known as the X type is used to illustrate "canopy last" type.

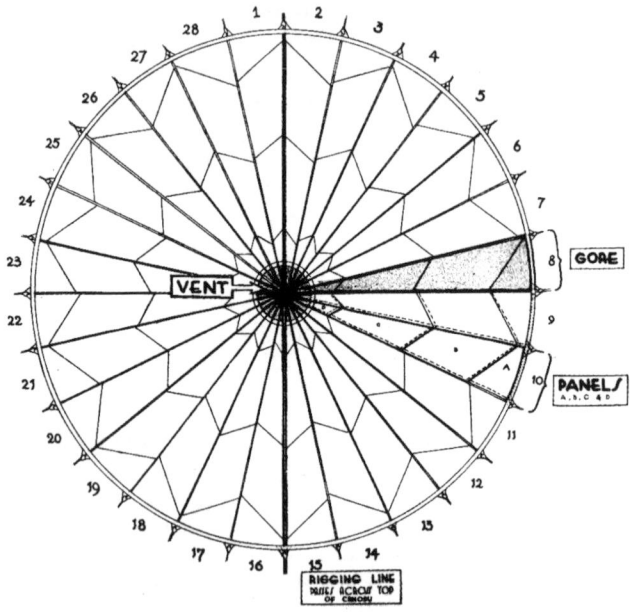

Fig. 47. The canopy.

19. *"Canopy First" Deployment*—In the case of the "canopy first" parachute one end of the static line is attached to a strong point in the aircraft. The other end is tied by light cord to the apex of the canopy which is stowed in a pack attached to the harness. The rigging lines are stowed in webbing loops on the inside of the pack. In fact the arrangement is very similar to that of the British pilot type manually operated parachute, except that the apex is not pulled out by the pilot parachute but is pulled out by the static line itself.

When the paratroop jumps, the static line is drawn taut and pulls the apex of the canopy out of the pack; the rest of the canopy follows in order from apex to periphery, the rigging lines are then withdrawn in order, periphery to lift webs, and finally the lift webs are withdrawn. The lift webs are the last part of the parachute to appear and when there is tension all the way from the paratroop to the strong point the tie at the apex breaks and the canopy starts to develop.

20. *"Canopy Last" Deployment.*—In the case of the "canopy last" parachute the parachute is stowed into a separate bag. This bag is firmly attached to the end of the static line and is held on to the paratroop's back by a light outer cover. The apex of

the canopy is tied to an extension of the static line inside the bag; the rigging lines are stowed in elastic loops on a loose flap attached to the mouth of the bag.

When the paratroop jumps, the static line is drawn taut and the bag is pulled away from the paratroop's back. As the bag is pulled away the parachute is pulled out of the bag in the order lift webs, rigging lines, periphery of canopy, apex of canopy. The apex of the canopy is the last part to appear, and when there is tension all the way from the man to the strong point the tie at the apex breaks and the canopy is free to develop.

21. The "canopy first" type is used by the U.S.A. Army and German Army for dropping from a door in the side of the fuselage; the "canopy last" type is used by the British Army and German Army for dropping through an aperture in the floor of the fuselage.

The apocryphal Napoleonic maxim that 'an army marches on its stomach' had an especial relevance to airborne forces, who went into an action without the stomach-filling support of field kitchen facilities. Typically, the airborne soldiers carried just one or two days of rations about their person, with supplementary supplies in airdropped containers. In the US forces, the 'K ration' provided the primary source of short-term (24-hour) nutrition, the three separately boxed packs in the ration delivering sustenance for breakfast, lunch and dinner; the three combined boxes provided just under 3,000 calories of energy. The following US military *Intelligence Bulletin* article reflects on how the diet of German airborne troops contributed to their physical and mental dynamism.

From *'Rations as a Factor in Paratroop Efficiency'* (June 1944)

It is popularly but wrongly supposed that German paratroopers are granted special ration privileges at all times. Membership in German parachute units (as in the case of U.S. Army parachute units) is on a voluntary basis, and in this connection the Germans put out a good deal of propaganda about special rations, to attract volunteers. The truth is that enemy paratroops receive special rations only just before actual parachute operations. When these soldiers are to go into combat as ordinary infantrymen, no additional rations are issued.

However, the specially planned rations that are given to German paratroopers prior to jumping (both in training and in combat) have a significance, the importance of which will not escape the intelligent U.S. fighting man. These rations include items which are not only attractive to the Germans, thereby building morale, but which will actually increase the physical stamina of the paratroop personnel. Incidentally, the special rations, creating a heartier appetite, lead to greater consumption of ordinary food; although the latter may be less attractive, they are energy-giving and naturally help to improve physical fitness.

White bread and dairy products, such as milk and fresh eggs, are considered real luxuries by the German soldiers; these items normally are not issued to troops of the other arms and services as part of the regular diet. On the day that a jump is to be made, German paratroopers are given the following, in addition to their normal ration:

> approx. .7 lb. white bread
> approx. .25 lb. crackers
> approx. .06 lb. butter
> approx. 1 pt. fresh milk
> 1 fresh egg

A ration of an entirely different kind is issued on days when long flights are to be made. The Germans have studied the nutritional benefits of specialized rations, and have concluded that on long flights regular rations sit too heavily on the stomach. The rations described below are issued only when two flights of two hours duration are to be made, or a single flight lasting four hours or more.

> approx. .16 lb. crystallized fruits
> approx. .25 lb. crackers
> approx. .01 lb. sugar
> approx. .04 lb. butter
> 1 bar of chocolate substitute

Analysis of this ration indicates that it contains an abundance of energy-giving foods which will sustain an individual without causing gastric discomfort.

The Germans have adopted an iron ration which is intended to last for a three-day period during operations. This emergency ration is similar to those developed by the United States and Great Britain. A ration of this bulk can easily be carried on the person, and provides the necessary "lift" for a man to carry out the most arduous tasks. It consists of:

- 2 cans of sausage
- 2 cans of cheese
- 1 bar of chocolate substitute
- 1 package of crackers
- 6 packages of chewing gum
- 1 package of lemonade powder
- 1 package of coffee mixed with sugar
- 1 tablet of solid fuel for heating

The iron rations are intended to make the German paratrooper self-sufficient for a limited period of time. Inclusion of the fuel tablet allows him to prepare a hot beverage, and yet maintain individual security precautions. This tablet burns for about 5 minutes, yielding a smokeless white flame 2 or 3 inches high.

CHAPTER 3

GLIDER AND AIRCRAFT DEPLOYMENT

G liders appear curious and cumbersome to modern eyes. Towed by powered aircraft to the release point, which was up to c. 5 miles from the landing zone (LZ), they thereafter glided their way to their objective inexorably dropping all the way. They were fragile under enemy fire, slow and easy to target, and their landings were at best hair-raising, at worst lethal. Because gliders had limited aerodynamic control, were highly susceptible to being blown off course, were often deployed at night, and by design had to skid-land in natural terrain (which ranged from a favourable flat field to a wing-smashing forest), casualties could be high upon landing – it was not unknown for all occupants to be killed or injured in a failed touch-down. But despite the risks, gliders offered some useful tactical possibilities. They facilitated the deployment of larger forces, with heavier equipment, than parachutes alone – a CG-4A Waco glider, for example, could carry 13 troops and equipment or a ¼-ton Jeep/vehicle/trailer or 75mm pack howitzer. By carrying a collective unit of troops, LZ dispersal could therefore, theoretically, be limited; parachute drops were notorious for scattering the soldiers far and wide. Gliders could be manufactured in large numbers at relative inexpense, and were therefore expendable, unlike costly powered aircraft. Gliders also had a silent approach (unlike paratrooper drop aircraft), meaning that they could maximize surprise. Finally, the occupants of gliders needn't necessarily have been through the complexities of parachute training (although many of them had), thus that a larger pool of troops were available for airborne ops.

The first manual presented below specifically relates to the Airspeed AS.51 or AS.58 Horsa glider, which could at maximum capacity take 30 fully armed troops. Some 3,600 of this British-built aircraft were constructed, and it was put to use not only by UK airborne forces, but also those of Canada, the United States and even India.

From *Pilot's Notes for Horsa Glider* (1944)

PART I
CONTROLS AND EQUIPMENT FOR PILOTS

INTRODUCTORY

1. The Horsa I is a high-wing, monoplane glider designed for transporting 25 troops with their equipment, or military equipment and light vehicles.

The main wheels of the tricycle undercarriage are jettisonable, and a landing skid protects the fuselage when making belly landings. Benches are fitted in the main cabin for the troops, and eight military equipment containers (with parachutes) are slung in cells, four on each side, under the wing. The pilot's cockpit in the nose seats two pilots side by side. Section 1 describes the pilot's controls and equipment, and other equipment with which the pilot should be familiar. Items of equipment shown in figs. 1 to 3 are numbered and these numbers appear in brackets in the text.

PNEUMATIC SYSTEM

2. **Compressed air.**—Three bottles, two outboard of the starboard pilot's seat, and one on the floor across the nose, supply compressed air for operating the flaps, wheel brakes, and undercarriage jettison release. A pressure gauge (12) is fitted. When fully ete cycles of flap operation and for subsequent normal braking on landing.

GLIDER CONTROLS

COCKPIT - GENERAL VIEW

Key to Fig. 1: 1. Flare release control; 2. Wheel brake lever; 3. Clear vision panels; 4. T.R.9D controls; 5. Lugs connecting port & starboard control column; 6. Locking pin for (5).

3. Primary controls are conventional and are normally interconnected by a locking pin (6) connecting two lugs (5) which projects through the front face of the well between the pilot's seats on the starboard side. To disconnect the starboard control column the locking wire should be pulled out and the pin withdrawn to the left by means of the plated tommy forming the head of the pin. The starboard hand-wheel can be removed by unscrewing the wing nut (18) securing it to its hub.

4. Rudder control.—bars (7) have tow straps and are adjustable for reach, on the ground, to any of five positions; they are permanently interconnected.

5. Elevator tab control.—The hand-wheel (23), mounted on the left of the control pedestal, operates in the natural sense.

6. Elevator tab indicator.—There is a mark on the cable drum which should be set opposite the arrow on the control pedestal for take-off.

Note: As the wheel can be rotated through approximately one full turn forward and backward from the neutral position, the take-off position should be checked by rotating the wheel back and forth about half a turn to ensure that when the mark is opposite the arrow the control is in the correct setting.

7. Flaps control.—The flaps are controlled by a lever (22) working in a quadrant forming the rear face of the control pedestal. The quadrant is marked UP, 40°, and FULL DOWN and the lever should be set to these positions only. Intermediate flap settings cannot be obtained. A spring in the quadrant enables the 40° position to be selected by feel; slight pressure is required to move the lever in either direction from this setting.

8. Air brakes.—The control levers (9) extend upwards, one at each side of the control pedestal; they are interconnected and are pulled back and down to apply the brakes; spring catches with release trigger grips are fitted to retain the levers in any desired setting.

9. Wheel brakes control.—A lever (8) spring catch and release-trigger grip, fitted on the port pilot's seat frame on his right, is pulled up to apply the brakes.

10. Undercarriage jettison release control.—A lever (21) with a red knob shaped to represent a wheel is fitted to starboard of the flap lever. It is retained in the LOCKED position by means of a spring locking pin; to release, the pin is withdrawn and the lever pushed down.

11. Undercarriage emergency jettison control.—Should the pilot's control fail to act there is a mechanical control on the aft face of No.5 bulkhead to starboard, with operating lever stowed alongside, for operation by the second pilot or by one of the troops.

12. Tow release control.—The tow release hooks in the leading edges of the wing centre-section are operated by a red lever (20) extending from the top of the control pedestal. The forward position is marked LOCKED and the rear position RELEASE.

13. Instruments.—The following are mounted on a panel above the control pedestal:- ASI (11), artificial horizon (15), rate of climb and descent indicator (16), altimeter (8) and a turn and bank indicator (l7). Above this panel is a narrower board carrying the air pressure gauge (12), a flying limitations plate (13) and an adjustable panel light (14), for which a dimmer switch (32) is on the switch panel to the left of the port pilot's seat.

14. Compass.—A compass (19) is mounted on a bracket extending from the starboard side of the control pedestal and a compass deviation card holder (10) is attached to the windscreen frame in line with the port pilot's wheel.

15. Mark II Tow cable angle indicator.—

(i) This indicator is similar to the Mark I – HOTSPUR – type having a horizontal bar (referred to in the Instrument Manual as the horizontal pointer) which moves up and down as the position of the glider, relative to the tug, rises and falls. On the Mk.II the vertical pointer, which pivots about its lower end, is connected to a gyro controlled artificial horizon unit

INSTRUMENT PANEL AND CONTROLS

Key to Fig. 2: 7. Port rudder bar; 8. Altimeter; 9. Air brake control lovers; 10. Compass deviation card; 11. A.S.I.; 12. Air pressure gauge; 13. Flying limitations plate; 14. Instrument panel light; 15. Artificial horizon; 16. Rate of climb and descent indicator; 17. Turn and bank indicator; 18. Wing nut securing starboard control wheel; 19. Compass; 20. Tow release control lever; 21. Undercarriage jettison control lever; 22. Flaps control lever; 23. Elevator tab control.

as well as to the cable angle mechanism. It indicates true angle of bank, or cable horizontal angle variation, or a combination of both, and indicates zero whenever the correct amount of bank is being applied.

(ii) In free flight, or on tow in the "high" tow position the cable angle measuring mechanism is out of action and the horizontal bar disappears from view at the top of the instrument. The vertical pointer continues to function, however, but being controlled by the artificial horizon mechanism only may be used in free flight to indicate angle of bank. For angles of bank in excess of 30° the response of the pointer decreases progressively, thus, at 90° bank, the pointer indicates 45° only.

(iii) The zero setting of the pointer is adjustable by means of the wing nut adjuster below the instrument this is turned in the opposite direction to that in which it is desired to rotate the pointer. The pointer can only be zeroed when flying in the low tow position with the cable angle mechanism working.

DOORS, SEATS AND COCKPIT EQUIPMENT

16. Pilot's entrance.—There is a door on the port side aft of the cockpit with an access ladder which is stowed in the main cabin; the door slides upwards and is secured by two latch fastenings which can be operated from inside or outside the glider. This door forms part of a larger door which opens outward about a hinge at its lower edge to form a ramp for the entry of light vehicles etc. From the main cabin the cockpit is reached through a central door in the bulkhead forming the front wall of the cabin.

17. Troop's entrances.—The troops use the door on the port side as well as a similar door on the starboard Bide aft of the wing.

18. Seats.—The pilot's seats are fixed and are provided with safety lap belts (33).

19. Hood.—The plastic hood affords a wide range of vision and there are two clear vision panels (3) one on each side of the windscreen; these spring up to open and catches are provided to retain them in this position.

20. Map case.—A container (3l) for maps, signal index cards etc. is attached to the front of the port pilot's seat frame.

21. Loading charts.—These are stowed in the main cabin about four feet aft of the cockpit bulkhead on the starboard side. On a board above this stowage are painted the tare weight, tare moment and the loading index number of the glider. Full instructions for use is given on the charts.

22. Thermos flasks.—A flask for the pilots is stowed at (24) on the shelf behind and outboard of the port pilot's head. Flask and ration containers for the troops are stowed below the seat benches.

25. Sanitary equipment.—A sanitary bottle for the pilots is stowed in clips on the forward face of the bulkhead outboard of the port pilot's seat back. There is also a sanitary tube for the use of the troops in the main cabin.

OPERATIONAL EQUIPMENT

24. Gun hatches.—There is a hatch in the roof of the main cabin, normally covered by a fabric panel with spring catches, as well as an underbody gun hatch in the tail; these are for use by machine gunners in the event of attack.

25. Equipment container release control.—The equipment containers are released by pull handles on the fuselage sides, at shoulder height, about two feet forward of the rear door line. each handle releases the group of four containers on the same side.

26. Landing flare release control.—There is a flare chute underneath the port pilot's seat. The handle (1) which is pulled up to release the flare, is on the right of the port pilots seat.

LIGHTING, RADIO & SIGNALLING EQUIPMENT

27. Radio.—There is a T.R.9D set installed with a remote control unit (4) for the pilots mounted on the left of starboard pilot's seat. The head-set jack socket for the port pilot is secured to the seat frame outboard of the seat.

28. Intercommunication.—The T.R.9D set provides inter-communications between the glider and tug pilots.

COCKPIT – PORT SIDE

29. Lights.—There is a fuse box (30) on the switch panel on the port fuselage aide by the pilot's seat. This panel carries a morsing key unit (28) with switches for downward Identification lights, a two-way switch (27) for navigation lights, two-way switch (29) for the cabin lights and a dimmer switch (32) for the instrument panel light. To enable the cabin lights to be used at night blackout curtains for the cabin windows are stowed in a container on the port forward face of the after bulkhead in the main cabin.

30. Torches.—Four electric torches are stowed in clips in the roof of the main cabin.

31. Signal pistol.—For use this fits into a discharge tube projecting from the floor outboard of the port pilot's seat. Stowage for cartridges (25) is provided on the fuselage side level with the port pilot's shoulder.

EMERGENCY EXITS & EQUIPMENT

32. Parachute exits.—The pilots should use the sliding door in the port side. The troops use this door as well as the door in the starboard side. The two gun hatches can also be used as parachute or crash exits should the main doors jam. To remove the main cabin gun hatch cover, pull string handles, unfasten spring catches and pull beams in.

33. First-aid kit.—This is stowed on the forward face of the rear bulkhead on the starboard side below the transverse seat.

PART II
HANDLING AND FLYING NOTES FOR PILOTS

1. INTRODUCTION

(i) These notes are for the guidance of pilots flying Horsa glider combinations. Tug aircraft pilots should also refer to Part III and the appropriate appendix thereto covering the tug aircraft used.

(ii) The method of signalling (intercom or visual) to be used between the glider and tug pilots, both on the ground and in the air, should be agreed and the code of visual signals to be used in emergency (or if intercom is not to be used) should be in accordance with the instructions laid down by the command concerned.

Note: It is of vital importance that glider and tug pilots shall agree and understand the code of signals to be used. The tug PILOT is CAPTAIN of the COMBINATION.

(iii) The directions in which glider and tug should turn after casting off should be in accordance with procedure laid down by the Command concerned and should be agreed by the pilots.

2. FLYING LIMITATIONS

(i) The maximum permissible weight is 15,250 lb.

Weight limitations applying to specific combinations are given in the appropriate tug aircraft appendices.

(ii) <u>Maximum permissible speeds</u> in m.p.h. I.A.S.

Towing	160 – (150 R.A.S.)
Diving	190
Flaps half down	110
Flaps fully down	100

Note

(i) The above limitations as well as the recommended handling speeds given in these notes are subject to any temporary restrictions which may be in force at the date of issue, or which may be Imposed from time to time by Special instruction.

(ii) The Rectified Airspeed (R.A.S.) given in brackets is for the use of tug pilots in converting to tug I.A.S.

3. POSITION ERROR CORRECTION

At all speeds the correction may be taken as 10 m.p.h. to be subtracted from A.S.I. reading.

4. FITNESS OF AIRCRAFT FOR FLIGHT

Ensure that the total weight and C.G. position are within the permitted limits. Heavy loads should in no ease be carried without calculating the C.G. position by means of the loading charts.

Rough guides to loading are:–

(a) Two pilots, or a first pilot and ballast in the second pilot's place, should be carried.

Note: Gliders must not be flown light without a second pilot or ballast in lieu.

(b) Any load should be disposed evenly about a point one third of the chord length aft of the leading edge at the wing root.

5. PRELIMINARIES

Before entering the cockpit:

(i) See that all passengers are seated and strapped in, and the load secured. Report the all-up weight to the tug pilot.

(ii) See that the glider is directly behind the tug and on the same heading, and that the nose wheel is straight.

On entering the cockpit:

(iii) Test operation of the tow release and see that the tow release control is left in the fully forward position.

(iv) See that the undercarriage jettison lever is in the correct position.

Note: On certain gliders the undercarriage is not jettisonable.

  (v) Check that all air bottles are turned on, and check pressure.–

    (a) Minimum for training (providing the under-carriage is not to be jettisoned) 100 lb/sq.in.

    (b) Minimum for operational use – 200 lb/sq.in.

 (vi) If used test inter-communication with tug. When line intercom is used the amplifier switch must be on at all times when on tow. A code of visual signals should, in any case, be agreed between the pilots for use in an emergency should the intercom fail.

(vii) Test all flying controls for full and free movement, and check that the wing nut on the starboard control wheel is secure.

(viii) see that the catches for retaining the clear vision panels in the open position operate properly.

6. PREPARATION FOR TAKE-OFF

  (i) Check list before take-off

Flaps	-	UP		
Air pressure	-	Minm.	100 lb.	(200 lb for operational flights)
Trim	-	Neutral		
Altimeter	-	Zero		
Brakes	-	Off		

 (ii) When ready to take-off instruct pilot by intercom to.–

    (a) Take up slack.

    (b) Take-off – when cable is nearly taut.

7. TAKE-OFF

  (i) Keep directly behind the tug.

 (ii) At an ample margin above stalling speed (see para 13) pull off gently and hold near the ground until tug takes off.

(iii) When the tug is clear of the ground, climb gently to a height which brings the tug end of the tow-rope approximately horizontal. Do not get higher than this.

(iv) If the Mk.II indicator is to be used, allowing three minutes after take-off for the gyro to erect, zero the pointer; this should be done with the tug flying straight and the glider central below the slip-stream (the instrument only functions in the low tow position).

8. UNDERCARRIAGE JETTISON

The undercarriage should not be jettisoned at less than 200 ft as it may bounce and hit the tail. In training conditions the undercarriage should only be dropped, when authority has been given for doing this, by the parachute method and should not be released at less than 200 ft or 115 mph IAS. Avoid jettisoning the undercarriage if the wind speed exceeds about 10 mph as it may be damaged if it lands with much drift; practice drops over runways or other hard surfaces should be avoided.

9. CLIMBING

During initial climb the best towing position is just above the tug, in such a position that the tug end of the tow-rope is in a line with the tug flight path.

10. BEST POSITION ON TOW

To obtain the maximum rate of climb and range it is of importance that once steady climbing conditions have been reached and in level flight, the glider shall maintain the correct position in relation to the tug flight path. These positions are as follows:–

(i) High Tow Position. Directly behind the tug and one half the wing span of the tug above it (with experience this position may be gauged by observing the relationship between the tug tailplane and mainplane) it is not sufficient to keep just clear of the slipstream.

(ii) Low Tow Position. Directly behind the tug and one half the wing span of the tug below it. This position is to be preferred, except during initial climb, for the following reasons:–

(a) The glider tends to maintain position more naturally than in the high tow position.

(b) The correct vertical position is such that the glider is just clear of the slipstream and can therefore be more precisely gauged.

NOTE

(i) In both high and low tow positions the glider should not be allowed to get more than one tug wing span above or below it, as otherwise cable drag becomes excessive.

(ii) The charts – Figs.1 & 2 – show the relationship between the salient features of tug aircraft, as seen from the glider when flying in the BEST and LIMIT positions on both high and low tow.

The true BEST and LIMIT positions will vary with tug loading and IAS so that the silhouettes, which are based on incidence angles at certain specific loadings and speeds, must be taken as a general guide only. Pilots will find the most comfortable high and low tow positions by experience and, as it is tiring to maintain one position for long periods, some variation is permissible provided, generally, that the outline of the tug remains between the positions depicted by the silhouettes marked BEST and LIMIT.

[. . .]

11. LEVEL FLIGHT

(i) Air brakes, when fitted, may be used for taking up slack.

(ii) On turns, keep directly behind (or slightly inside) the tug.

(iii) Cloud Flying.– If cloud is entered the glider pilot should release tow immediately unless a tow cable angle indicator is fitted and authority has been given for blind flying.

12. BLIND FLYING (using Mk.II Tow cable angle indicator)

(i) On tow fly in low tow position; correction should be made with the elevator and ailerons assisted F.S/3 as necessary by rudder. Inclination of the vertical pointer indicates departure of the glider from its correct angle of bank and the pointer should be "pushed" gently back to zero with the ailerons.

As soon as the pointer reaches the zero position a touch of opposite aileron should be applied to stop the pointer moving and to prevent the glider overshooting its correct position. This technique applies equally in level flight and when turning, climbing or descending. Movement of the horizontal bar indicates corresponding departure of the glider from its correct vertical position which should be corrected by pushing gently on the elevator control so as to push the bar back to the zero position. In rough weather some oscillation of the horizontal bar occurs (due to surging of the cable) but the vertical position of the glider is indicated by the mean of the limits of oscillation and no attempt to correct the oscillation is necessary.

(ii) In free flight. The vertical pointer can be used in a similar manner to an artificial horizon to indicate angle of bank, correction being applied by aileron as when on tow.

13. CASTING-OFF

(i) This should be done in level flight with the glider level with or above the tug. Except in emergency, do not cast off from below the tug. Speed should be at least 90 mph IAS and after casting off the tug will turn as prescribed.

(ii) If take-off is abandoned, either by the tug or by the glider pilot the rope should be released and the glider should then turn as prescribed.

14. STALLING

(i) Stalling speeds in mph IAS.

	Lightly loaded	Fully loaded
Flaps up	54	69
Flaps down	43	55

(ii) If the stall is approached quickly, or if the control column is held right back after a slow approach, one wing may drop gently.

15. GLIDING

(1) The following speeds in mph IAS (with undercarriage) are recommended:

	Light	Heavy
Flaps up	70	85
Flaps half down	65	75

(ii) With flaps fully down the glide path is extremely steep. Flaps can he raised to the half down position without appreciable sink; it is not necessary to increase speed.

16. APPROACH AND LANDING

(i) Up to half flap may be used on the cross wind approach to regulate height.

(ii) Make the final turn towards the landing ground with half flap and when sure of getting into the landing ground, lower the flaps fully.

(iii) The glide path with flaps fully down is steep, and care is necessary, especially in strong winds, not to get too far downwind. Flaps may be raised to the half down position if undershooting. Flaps mist not be raised fully at normal flaps down approach speeds, and even if speed is increased in order to raise them fully, this will not correct undershooting at this stage of the approach.

(iv) Recommended speeds for final straight approach, with flaps fully down are:
Light   60 mph IAS
Heavy   75 to 80 mph IAS

(v) Flatten out and land on the main wheels in a slightly tail down attitude, lower the aircraft gently onto the nose wheel and then, when all three wheels are on the ground, apply brakes.

Note: the brake action is not differential.

Airlanding was typically used when an airfield was already secured and troops were being flown in as reinforcements, along with the heavier equipment that could be used to bolster combat strength. Airlanded soldiers might be little more than regular infantry placed aboard an aircraft, but they would still need to have solid combat skills, not least because they would usually be deployed into the thick of the fighting, even if they were not in the vanguard.

Certain aircraft came to dominate the airlanding roles. On the Allied side, the C-47 Skytrain (or the Dakota in RAF or RAAF parlance) and its specialist paratrooper variant, the C-53 Skytrooper, were the true workhorses of airborne warfare and of airborne logistics in general, known for their reliability and capacious interiors – the C-53 could hold 28 fully equipped combat troops. For the Germans, the trimotor Junkers Ju 52 was the signature aircraft, although at 17 troops its capacity was significantly below that of the C-47. Regardless of the type of aircraft, however, such transport aircraft were slow beasts, vulnerable to both anti-aircraft fire and enemy fighters, so for those deploying them localized air supremacy was vital.

The following manual explains a few of the key principles of airlanding and glider operations, from the aircraft suitable for purpose to the equipment that was carried aboard. It was published by the War Office in mid 1945, and produced in cooperation between the Imperial General Staff and the Chief of the Air Staff.

From *Airborne Airtransported Operations* (1945)

CHAPTER 3.– AIRTRANSPORTED FORCES

"The best thing about travel is that it teaches what are the places that are not worth seeing."

(M. Pierre Benoit.)

Summary

146. This Chapter 3 deals with the points peculiarly applicable to the army (less airborne formations) in an airtransported role. Though the principles of air movement are similar for both airborne and airtransported forces, additional requirements are introduced when a tactical airtransported formation is flown by air. These are:–

(a) The equipping of units with airportable equipment.

(b) The training of troops in movement by air. In addition to staff duties and movement discipline this includes dismantling, loading, lashing, unloading and reassembly of equipment at maximum speed.

(c) An increased ground organization to control the fly-in and fly-out of a large number of transport aircraft and to deal with the loading and unloading of supplies and equipment which may require dismantling and which may be beyond the unit or sub-unit resources.

147. The increasing ability to move by air troops and equipment in tactical units is giving to the army a new role and new responsibilities. A third method of approach to the battle area has become available. It entails duties which become as much a part of Staff Duties as movement by land or sea. Training and intelligent interest must prevent movement by air from becoming a mystery to be interpreted only by a specialized headquarters "high priest." Although the working out of the details for a move is largely the responsibility of the Q Staff, the handling and employment of airtransported troops is an essential basic duty of all staff officers. In the division of army Staff Duties there is little difference between a move by road or sea with its order of move and a move by air with its order of flight. The principal differences between a tactical move by sea and by air lie in the restricted loading capacities of aircraft and the greater dependence on weather. The possibilities for independent initiative and improvisation on the part of airtransported units make it particularly necessary that general information on matters of air transport support must be the concern of all personnel; in this way the real and essential co-operation with the air force at all levels can be achieved. Training and combined rehearsals are important means to this end.

[. . .]

Aircraft

149. Transport aircraft

(a) The two-engined Dakota (C-47) is the transport aircraft with which the army as a whole is primarily concerned in an airtransported role. The equipment with which an airtransported formation or the airtransported echelon of a normal infantry division can be equipped is at present, therefore, mainly controlled by the loading capacity of the Dakota with its average payload of 5,500 lbs. Other aircraft such as the American Commando (C-46) transport aircraft (9,000 lbs payload) have increased payload, but these are normally available only for special units under special circumstances.

For a tactical role airtransported forces require a tactical transport aircraft having a maximum loading capacity for awkward loads such as vehicles and requiring the minimum landing facilities in the forward areas. The Dakota is at present the nearest approach to these requirements and in addition is the best all purpose aircraft for the roles of a glider tug and a parachute aircraft.

(b) Some four-engined transport aircraft are capable of carrying larger equipment with less need for dismantling than the Dakota (C-47) as well as a larger payload. The increased requirements, however, in landing facilities such as surface and length of runway make their tactical employment in the forward areas unlikely unless good airfields are captured in the early stages of an operation. They are therefore normally employed for strategic and administrative moves.

150. The employment of gliders

Normally airtransported units travel in powered aircraft, but gliders will have to be employed for landing in areas where trips or airfields are not already available. They will be employed only when powered aircraft cannot land since they are normally an extravagant use of airlift. They are used mainly for the airlanding units of an airborne formation in air assault and follow-up roles. Their employment with airtransported forces will usually be for lifting engineer units for the purpose of preparing airstrips for powered transport aircraft.

Assuming adequate landing facilities, it is practicable for gliders to land on landing zones while their transport tugs land simultaneously on airstrips. This will increase the speed of build-up, but will increase the complexity of the plan and the ground organization required since their respective landing areas may be separated by several miles. Moreover, the payload of the aircraft as a tug will probably be less than its normal payload and may be entirely sacrificed.

The Horsa and Hadrian (CG4A) are the most common types of gliders. They have a payload of 6,900 lbs and approximately 4,000 lbs respectively and for awkward sized equipment the Horsa has slightly worse and the Hadrian slightly better loading characteristics than the Dakota (C47). The Hamilcar has both an increased payload (about 17,000 lbs) and a considerable increased loading aperture. The allotment of Hamilcars to airtransported units will, however, be exceptional.

Airtransported Units and Airportable Equipment

151. Broadly, there are two main categories of airtransported units:–

(a) Units whose normal equipment is airportable.

(b) Units whose equipment has been modified or exchanged to make them airportable for a particular airtransported operation.

152. Equipment is airportable in varying degrees. Its degree of airportability represents the time taken in loading and unloading, and affects the time of turn-round of the aircraft over a given period. It affects the speed with which units can get into action after landing, and it affects the size of the ground organization required to load and unload and to dismantle and reassemble if this work is beyond unit or sub-unit resources.

153. The word airportable may be misleading unless related to the particular aircraft concerned and the number of man-hours required for loading and unloading. For tactical employment there is a limit of time and effort which can be accepted, above which movement by air becomes administrative or freight transportation.

The degrees of airportability may be distinguished as:–

(a) Equipment which can be loaded without dismantling and without loading aids by unit personnel. For the Dakota (C47) examples are jeeps, trailers, mortars and artillery such as 3.7-how, 75-mm hows, 25-pr Mk 3 carriage.

(b) Equipment which requires to be dismantled for loading but which requires no lifting aids and which in the case of vehicles can, when dismantled, be driven into the aircraft.

For such equipment units can normally carry out their own loading. Examples in the case of the Dakota (C47) are the 25-pdr Mk 1 carriage, 40-mm Bofors, the airportable 15-cwt truck 4 × 4 and the ¾.-ton weapon carrier 4 × 4.

(c) Equipment which requires dismantling and lifting aids for unloading and reassembly in the forward area, and may require more than one aircraft. Vehicles which require wheel dismantling, such as 3-ton lorries and the larger tractors for airfield construction are examples. Normally, the handling of this type of equipment is beyond unit resources. The transport by air of such equipment increases the organization required for air movement.

Since the airfields must be kept clear at all times, equipment in a dismantled state will have to be transported some distance between the aircraft and the areas where dismantling and reassembly can be carried out. Special detachments may also be required at both base and forward airfields to handle such equipment. The need for quick dismantling makes it essential that particular care is taken to keep the joints and bolts of such equipment free from corrosion and rust. ·

154. To render equipment airportable in any of these categories, modifications may be required either to enable it to be loaded without dismantling or to simplify dismantling. Such modifications have to be done as long before the move as possible. In as many cases as possible the modifications will eventually be included by manufacturers in production.

155. Formations in an airtransported role inevitably divide into a light element which can move by air with comparative case and heavier elements, which if possible follow by land or sea or some parts of which may follow by air when greater airlift and landing facilities are available. The loading and weight restrictions particularly affect tracked and armoured vehicles: unless aircraft are available into which they can be loaded without dismantling they are unsuited to an airtransported role.

Being a glider pilot was one of the most precarious roles in military aviation. Not only did the pilot have to fly a large, unpowered and sometimes overloaded aircraft, but he also had to do it in combat conditions. Landings were thumping and dangerous, plus once down the air crew (gliders were typically two-man aircraft) would find themselves effectively becoming infantry soldiers, often deep behind enemy lines. In British circles, the glider pilots were sometimes known as 'total soldiers', on account of their required versatility.

For such reasons, glider pilot training was highly demanding. In the UK, many pilots were, from 1942, trained within the Glider Pilot Regiment, part of the British Army but with a naturally close liaison with the RAF. In the United States, pilots gained instruction through the glider programme delivered by the USAAC/USAAF. Notably, all the US pilots were volunteers and all came from enlisted ranks, and some 5,500 were trained up during the war years. The aircraft they were destined to man was principally the Waco CG-4A, and sections of the instruction manual are here reproduced.

From *Pilot's Flight Operating Instructions for Army Model CG-4A Glider (British Model Hadrian)* (1942)

SECTION I
DESCRIPTION AND OPERATION

A US Army Air Force Waco CG-4A-WO glider.

1. GENERAL.

The model CG-4A glider is a 15-place high wing land monoplane built in accordance with the Army Air Forces Specification No. 1025-2. It has a fabric-covered steel tube fuselage, and a 2-spar, plywood to the rear spar, fabric-covered wing.

2. WING.

a. GENERAL DESCRIPTION.

(1) High wing of 2-spar wooden construction, plywood covering to the rear spar, and fabric-covered throughout. It is externally braced by metal struts with fabric fairing. The wing has a span of 83 feet 8 inches and an area of 851. 5 square feet.

Fig. 2. Cockpit and flying controls.

1. Tab Controls	10. Cockpit Light
2. Tow Release	11. Sliding Windows
3. Dual Control Column	12. Ventilators
4. Fuse Panel	13. Instrument Panel
5. Recognition Light Control Box	14. Interphone Jack Box
6. Spoiler Control Handle	15. Nose Lock Release
7. Brake Pedals	16. Pedal Adjustment Lever
8. Interphone Microphone	17. Rudder Pedals
9. Load Adjuster	

3. EMPENNAGE.

a. GENERAL DESCRIPTION.

(1) All tail surfaces are of wood and plywood construction with wooden leading edge and fabric covering.

(2) Trim tabs are provided for both elevator and rudder.

4. FUSELAGE.

GENERAL DESCRIPTION.–The fuselage is of welded steel tube construction with fairings of wooden sections supporting the fabric covering.

5. TAIL WHEEL.

The tail wheel is nonsteerable. In tactical operations, where it is necessary to tow or retrieve the glider over rough terrain, soft dirt, or sand, the tail wheel will be secured in a tow dolly and the glider towed backwards. An adequate tow dolly may be fabricated from a serviceable jettisonable gear. Only under extreme emergency should the glider be towed by attaching a towline to the tow gear release mechanism.

6. UNDERCARRIAGE.

a. The design incorporates two different types of undercarriages, the first of which is an articulated tripod consisting of a vee strut in an approximately horizontal plane and a spring oleo shock absorber in approximately the vertical plane. This type gear equipped with hydraulic brakes and pneumatic tires is referred to as the "training gear."

b. The second type undercarriage is a "tactical" jettisonable gear which can be jettisoned after take-off and consists of a reinforced axle with 27-inch wheel and tire assembly, without brakes. When the jettison gear is used, the landing gear release mechanism will be checked thoroughly for operation two or three times prior to take-off.

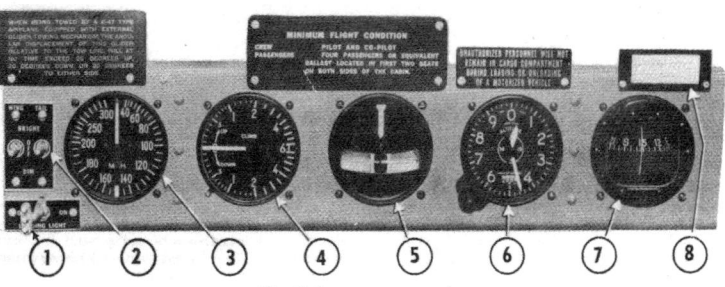

Fig. 3. Instrument panel.

1. Landing Light Switch
2. Navigation Light Switch
3. Airspeed Indicator
4. Rate of Climb Indicator
5. Bank and Turn Indicator
6. Altimeter
7. Compass
8. Compass Compensation Card

7. CONTROLS (FLIGHT).

a. The central control system consists of dual controls. Control of ailerons and elevators is obtained by two wheels mounted on an inverted "vee" column, hinged at the top of the cockpit. The right-hand column may be removed if desired in which case the lefthand column may be swung over from the pilot to the copilot. Individual rudder pedals are provided which are adjustable fore and aft. The pilot's pedals are equipped with the conventional toe brakes.

b. Trim tabs are actuated by cranks above the pilot's head at the center of the compartment. A round plate behind each trim tab crank handle gives full direction for trimming the glider about the three flight axes. It is inadvisable for the glider pilot to look at the trim tab controls to determine the direction to turn crank for desired trim, during flight. The direction the trim tab is turned should be memorized by the pilot.

c. JETTISONABLE (TACTICAL) GEAR CONTROLS.–An overhead lever is provided to release the tactical gear.

d. SPOILER CONTROLS.–At the pilot's left and the copilot's right are the spoiler levers which, when pulled, extend the spoilers. These spoilers decrease lift, increase the gliding angle, and raise the sinking speed.

e. NOSE RELEASE CONTROL.–Directly between the pilot and copilot is located the nose release lever, which is wired closed during training or while carrying troops. This lever is used to release two latches located in the lower rear corners of the pilot's compartment. It is operated only when necessary to load or unload equipment which cannot pass through the doors located at the rear of the cargo compartment.

8. FUSELAGE EQUIPMENT.

a. GENERAL DESCRIPTION.–Fuselage equipment consists of seats, safety belts, tie-down fittings, nose lifting mechanism, flight report holder, data case, fire extinguisher, first-aid kits and mooring kit.

(1) COCKPIT SEATS.–The cockpit seats are non-adjustable; that is, are mounted directly to the fuselage structure.

(2) When used as a troop transport, removable wooden benches are fastened longitudinally in the fuselage.

(3) D-rings are provided at the lower ends of all vertical tubing members along the sides of the cargo compartment to provide for the lashing down of the cargo load.

(4) The nose lifting mechanism is used to automatically raise the nose (pilots' compartment) of the glider, by means of a ¼-ton reconnaissance car, located in the cargo compartment. The pilot or copilot must pull the nose release lever, and both these men must be out of the pilots' compartment before the nose lifting mechanism can be operated. T. 0. No. 09-40CA-5 covers the loading and unloading of a "jeep."

9. EMERGENCY EXIT.

a. Emergency doors are located halfway between cockpit and entrance doors.

b. Make absolutely certain that placard, with complete instructions on operation of emergency doors, located in cabin of glider, is carefully read.

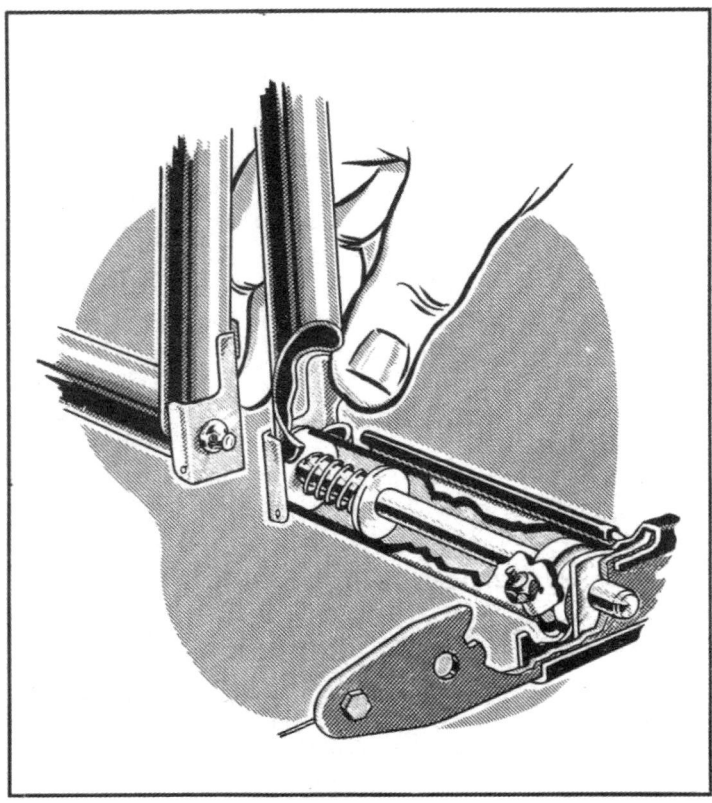

Fig. 4. Pedal adjustment.

SECTION II
GENERAL INSTRUCTIONS

1. PREFLIGHT INSPECTION.

a. GENERAL.–The pilot shall satisfy himself that the following inspection has been made and everything is satisfactory before take-off.

    (1) All flight instruments will be inspected in accordance with the General Inspection for all airplanes.

    (2) Before all flights, check that lock handles for the nose section at the front of the cargo compartment are definitely engaged.

(3) Check security of tail brace struts and wires. Check wires for tension.

(4) Check tactical landing gear to make sure gear is locked in place, and that release lever will actuate both hooks,' locking gear in place.

(5) Check to see that spoilers are in "CLOSED" position.

(6) Try all controls to make sure that external locks have been removed and full movement is unrestricted.

(7) Check tow release controls on both glider and tow plane as well as tow release attachment and metering pins.

(8) Set altimeter to read the same as towship altimeter at sea level altitude, if on a cross country mission. If operating and landing on the same airport, set altimeter at zero, or ground level.

(9) If radio communication is used, check radio with towplane. If intercommunication is installed, check with towplane and other glider, if on double tow.

(10) Check the loading of the glider for the "CENTER OF GRAVITY" position. In minimum flying condition (pilot and copilot) 600 pounds of ballast should be provided.

2. FLIGHT INSTRUCTIONS.

a. Fasten safety belt.

b. Adjust ventilators for circulation of air in front cockpit.

c. TAKE-OFF.–Set trim tab controls to neutral marks. After towplane has started its run and when glider has attained take-off speed, the glider should be pulled off carefully, and maintained from then on approximately 10 feet higher than the towplane. The pilot should attempt to keep the nose skids from touching the ground or runway on take-off. If this happens, hold the control column back to lighten the load on the skids as much as possible. When the glider is equipped with a jettisonable gear with parachute assembly, the gear should not be jettisoned until at least 400 feet of altitude is reached.

d. APPROACH AND LANDING.

(1) Spoilers may be utilized as desired to control gliding angle and sinking speed. Extreme caution should be exercised when using spoilers on the turn toward the landing strip. Spoilers should be applied with caution during the end of the landing approach, since full application results in a high sinking speed.

(2) The procedure for contacting the ground will be similar with all types of landing gear. If the landing gear has been jettisoned and landing is to be made on skids, it is desirable to land in a near level attitude, permitting

all skids to touch simultaneously. However, little or no damage will result if landed in a nose-high, three-point attitude. After ground contact is made, pilot will have very little control of the glider but should attempt to keep it straight ahead by use of the rudder. Average stop on sod terrain will be approximately 50 yards.

(3) Most missions will be planned using the hydraulic training type landing gear. Contact will be made in a three-point attitude, whenever possible. With this gear brakes are available for slowing the glider or steering it on ground run. Should a short stop be necessary, pilot will apply full brakes, ease control column forward until nose skids touch, then hold in a forward position with full brakes applied. On sod terrain a stop can be made in approximately 50 yards.

(4) If landing is made on the tactical jettisonable landing gear, a long roll can be expected. Contact with the ground will be identical to that used for the training type gear, and if a short run is desired, pilot will immediately push forward on control and attempt to stop by using nose skids.

(5) When the glider is used to carry the jeep, the nose latch should not be released until glider has come to a complete stop. When nose latch is released, pilot and copilot will immediately leave their seats and go out of the glider through the emergency exit door. When a jeep is carried with training type landing gear, it will be necessary to prop up the tail of the glider and hold the nose in contact with the ground before the unloading operation. After jeep has been unloaded the tail will be eased back to the ground to prevent damaging the "A" frame or tail cone. Only authorized personnel will remain in cargo section during the loading or unloading of a mechanized vehicle.

(6) TO OPERATE THE PARACHUTE. (For gliders equipped with deceleration parachutes only.) Note: The parachute will not be operated until the glider has released the towline and is in free flight. The parachute should not be opened when free flight indicated air speed is under 75 or above 140 mph.

(a) Upon approach to the landing area the parachute can be opened to attain an increased rate of descent. This is accomplished by pulling the parachute opening handle which is located in the nose section immediately to the right of the center line of the glider. The parachute control handles are equipped with a safety device to prevent the release handle being pulled before the parachute opening handle.

(b) After the parachute has been opened the copilot should be prepared for a signal from the pilot to release the parachute from the glider should such action be necessary.

(c) When approach to the landing area is made at a low altitude and high rate of speed the parachute may be opened at glider indicated air speeds of 80 to 140 mph to reduce forward speed of the glider.

(d) When approach is made to the landing area at a high altitude the parachute may be opened at a maximum indicated air speed of 140 mph to obtain an increased rate of descent. The rate of deceleration and loss of altitude are dependent upon the velocity and attitude of the glider at the time the parachute is opened.

(e) The rate of descent as shown in table I can be expected while the parachute is opened. (See table I.) Note: With a moderate pull up to level flying position the glider can be decelerated from 150 to 75 mph glider indicated air speed in 30 seconds with a loss in altitude of approximately 500 feet.

(f) Because of the higher rate of descent when the parachute is used, additional care must be taken in flaring out the glider path when making contact with the ground. In training, the parachute should be released from the glider before the tail wheel touches the ground or just before the glider comes to a stop, so that the parachute is not damaged by being dragged over the ground.

Miles per Hour Indicated Air Speed	Feet per Minute With Parachute Open
150	4200
140	3600
130	3000
120	2500
110	2000
100	1500
90	1150
80	800
70	700

The above table is applicable at sea level. An addition in rate of descent of approximately 2 percent will be attained per 1000 feet above sea level.

SECTION III
SPECIAL INSTRUCTIONS

1. LIMITATIONS OF FLYING AND FLYING CHARACTERISTICS.

Flying characteristics are dependent upon the towing airplane. The stalling speed of this ship fully loaded is approximately 60 mph indicated air speed. Spinning is prohibited. If a spin inadvertently develops, attempt a normal recovery.

No acrobatics should be undertaken in this type of craft.

Do not exceed a diving speed of 150 mph indicated. As elevator and rudder loads become quite heavy at high speeds, use trim tabs whenever possible.

2. EMERGENCY LANDING AT SEA.

a. PREPARATION FOR DITCHING

(1) Pilot warns crew as soon as he determines that ditching is necessary.

(2) Pilot instructs crew to jettison all doors and use bayonets to cut out exits in the roof or sides of the glider.

(3) Pilot instructs crew to throw all loose unnecessary equipment overboard.

(4) Pilot instructs crew to keep safety belts fastened until landing is accomplished.

(5) Copilot should knock out side windshield panel, unfasten parachute harness, make sure his safety belt is buckled, and then relieve the pilot of the controls so that he may accomplish the same.

b. DITCHING

(1) A tail-low landing should be made, flying the glider at minimum speed.

(2) In a wind below 25 mph velocity, land along the swell. In a wind about 25 mph velocity, land as near into the wind as possible and angle onto the upslope of the swell, according to conditions involved.

c. AFTER DITCHING

(1) The glider should be abandoned as shown in Fig. 6.

(2) All personnel should climb onto the wings of the glider as these sections will remain afloat for several hours. Precautions should be taken to prevent puncturing holes in the skin of the wing surfaces, as this will decrease the length of time the wing panels will remain afloat.

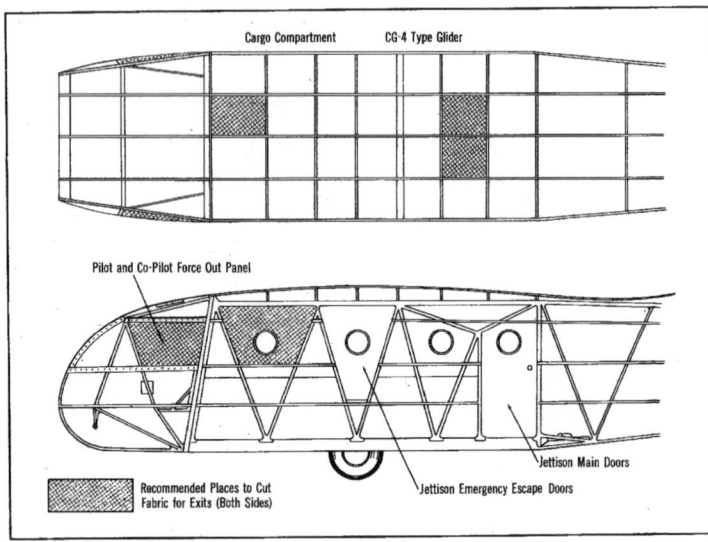

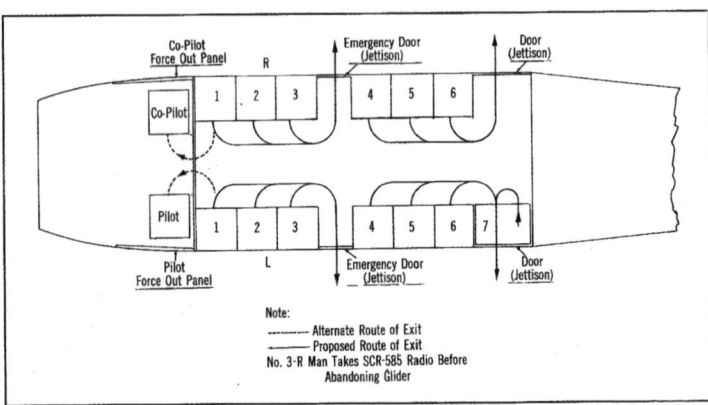

Fig. 7. Method of abandoning CG-4A glider.

SECTION IV
WEIGHT DATA

1. WEIGHTS.

	Jettisoned gear	*Training Gear*
Gross weight	7500 lb	7500 lb
Weight empty	3790 lb	3900 lb
Useful load	3710 lb	3600 lb
Wing loading	8.81 lb/sq ft	8.81 lb/sq ft

CAUTION

This glider must not be flown at less load than the following: pilot and copilot, four passengers or their equivalent weight located on the first two seats, each side, of the cargo compartment. For actual weight distribution in this glider, refer to the Handbook of Weight and Balance,

2. ALTERNATE LOADING.

a. To reduce the possibility of overloading CG-4A gliders prior to towing, the following restrictions will be observed:

b. Any CG-4A glider gross weight condition which exceeds the design condition of 7,500 pounds is to be considered as an operational emergency measure.

c. The CG-4A glider is never to be flown at a greater gross weight than 9,000 pounds.

d. The maximum permissible indicated air speeds at various gross weights is to be in accordance with table I below.

Glider Gross Weight	Maximum Permissible Calibrated Indicated	Maximum Permissible Glider Indicated Air Speed
7,500 lb	150 mph	158 mph
8,000 lb	143 mph	151 mph
8,500 lb	135 mph	143 mph
9,000 lb	128 mph	135 mph

Due to the location of the pitot tube on the CG-4A glider nose section, the glider airspeed instrument indicates air speeds approximately 8 mph higher than the calibrated indicated air speed.

A calibrated indicated air speed of 150 mph should not be exceeded under any glider gross weight condition, due to the possibility that windshield panels may blow in, and other failures may occur.

e. The glider center of gravity is to be maintained between the limits of 25 to 33.5 percent m.a.c. However, with a center of gravity of 30 to 31 percent m.a.c., it will be possible to keep the glider off the forward skids during the initial part of the take-off. With the glider loaded to emergency gross weights, satisfactory lateral, directional, and longitudinal control and trimming characteristics will be experienced. At the higher emergency gross weights, the glider will react somewhat sluggishly in towed flight.

f. Landing rolls of approximately 2,000 to 3,000 feet are to be expected at the higher emergency gross weights, even with full application of brakes.

g. Take-offs will be normal except for longer ground rolls and higher take-off speeds as the gross weight is increased.

3. SPECIAL LOADING INSTRUCTIONS.

a. TO LOAD THE ¼-TON TRUCK (JEEP).

(1) Unlatch and raise nose section, pulling cable so that the door check slides back along the rod to hold the door fully open.

(2) Let down ramps.

(3) Back in with car.

(4) Engage cable at rear of car.

(5) Lower nose section and lock in position.

(6) Move car forward to place initial tension in rear cable.

(7) Depress the springs of car by placing the weight of four men on the front bumper and tie down to shackle (D-ring) fittings using ½-inch rope.

(8) Install wheel chocks.

(9) Lash the rear end of the jeep in the same manner as in (7) above.

b. TO LOAD THE 75 MM. HOWITZER.

(1) Push Howitzer into cargo compartment, in the same way as the jeep, with the muzzle pointing aft.

(2) Lash securely to prevent fore and aft and vertical motions.

(3) Locate ammunition in accordance with flight adjuster and lash securely in place.

CAUTION

DO NOT ATTEMPT FLIGHT WITHOUT FIRST CHECKING BALANCE WITH FLIGHT ADJUSTER. (SEE HANDBOOK OF WEIGHTS AND BALANCE AN 01-1-40.)

4. UNLOADING INSTRUCTIONS.

a. UNLOADING JEEP.–The design of the glider is such that unloading may be accomplished in a matter of seconds with proper cooperation and training of the crew. The sequence of unloading is as follows:

CAUTION

Do not release the nose until the glider is completely stopped.

(1) The pilot shall trip the down lock holding the nose section closed and the copilot shall slash the tiedown rope on the front of the jeep.

(2) At the same time two of the crew members shall slash the rear tie-down ropes and free the jeep.

(3) When the nose section is released, the copilot goes back to the driver's seat of the jeep and the pilot rides out on the jeep hood.

(4) The jeep driver shall then drive forward, thereby opening the nose section by means of the ¼-inch cable attached to the tow hook of the jeep. (Ramps will fall into position automatically.)

(5) When nose section has been pulled to a horizontal position, a lanyard fixed to the structure shall trip the release mechanism and the structure will be held in this position by means of the automatic check attached to the cable.

b. UNLOADING 75 MM. GUN.

(1) Release nose down locks.

(2) Remove or cut lashings.

(3) Raise nose section by hand and lower ramps.

(4) Roll Howitzer out.

CHAPTER 4

AT THE DROP ZONE AND LANDING ZONE

One of the most dangerous moments of an entire airborne operation was that when the paratroopers leapt from the aircraft or when gliders made their final approach and landing. The dangers were painfully revealed to the Germans during Operation *Merkur* (*Mercury*), the invasion of Crete in May 1941. During the initial parachute drops, large numbers of German paratroopers were shot in their harnesses either as they descended to the ground or shortly after they landed, as they struggled awkwardly to free themselves from their parachute lines. (The design of the German parachute meant that the *Fallschirmjäger* could not carry a rifle or submachine gun at the ready during the descent; it therefore took him crucial moments after landing before he was combat active.) Large numbers of paratroopers sustained lower-leg and hip injuries as they hit the ground, the awkward landing characteristics of the RZ parachutes making unholy alliance with Crete's jagged volcanic landscape. Numbers of paras dropped into the sea off the Cretan coast, drowning while tangled in silk and line. The glider and airlanding forces had it no easier. Many of the gliders were torn apart as they ploughed through woodland groves or across sharp rock. Those that came to a successful rest were often hit within seconds by enemy small-arms and mortar fire; on occasions, New Zealander and Australian troops simply sat and waited for each paratrooper to emerge from the glider door, gunning them down in turn. Several Ju 52s were hit and destroyed by anti-aircraft fire even before men had leapt from the door.

By 1942, given the well-documented risks of airborne operations, much thought was given to ways of reducing the risk. This chapter focus on texts that address these issues, and which provide the requisite guidelines for deployment at the DZs and LZs. The first of the excerpts is from a document sent by the RAF No. 38 Wing, a formation that would go on to support parachute operations for Operation *Market Garden*, to the British Army Co-operation Command, a body formed in 1940 to facilitate inter-operability between the RAF and the Army.

From *'Tactics adopted for Paratroop dropping'* (1942)

From:- Headquarters, No. 38 Wing.
To:- Headquarters, Army Co-operation command.
Date:- 16th June 1942.
Ref:- 38W/S.1/14/Air.

SECRET.
TACTICS ADOPTED FOR PARATROOP DROPPING.

1. With reference to your S.139/3/Air.f, dated 7th June, 1942 the tactics and training requirements so far adopted in paratroop dropping may be summarized as follows:—

Daylight Attack.

2. In certain circumstances where reasonable air superiority has been obtained, the paratroops may be dropped in daylight. It may be assumed that in the Western theatre of war a full fighter escort will be essential and the dominating requirements are therefore follows:—

  (i) To concentrate parachute forces as much as possible so that cover can be given with the minimum number of fighter aircraft This means formation flying, flying by main units stepped up in height on the flight towards the objectives, and by sub-units on parallel courses over the dropping zone. To achieve this units require training in quick assembly in the vicinity of the base aerodrome after take-off. (It is noticeable that Squadrons today have great difficulty in doing this. The old practice of the leader flying a wide circle and subsequent aircraft getting into position by cutting in on a much shorter course is not now understood.)

  (ii) Formation Flying.

  (iii) Accenture timing at specified heights over the main assembly rendezvous.

  (iv) Correct navigation to the final rendezvous.

  (v) Losing height and flying in a mass on parallel courses to the dropping zone.

It must be specially impressed upon navigators that in order to drop accurately, they must correct any navigational errors some miles before reaching the dropping zone, and must have as accurate mental picture of landmarks and features on the last part of the run in, so that this can be carried out without looking at the map and with full concentration on timing and country recognition.

Night Dropping.

3. This applies to drops by moon-light or at first light when the approach is in darkness. In this case, formation flying cannot be adopted Pilots therefore take

off at as short intervals as possible and navigate to a main rendezvous where main units may be stepped up in height and sub-units separated by short intervals of timing. From there each aircraft flies independently by dead reckoning to the final rendezvous, where again small intervals of timing between the sub-units are allowed for. From the final rendezvous, aircraft fly in to dropping zone individually following the exact route laid down in the flight plan which is selected to follow series of easily recognisable land marks. The approach is made at a height suitable for low map reading, i.e. 1000 to 1500 ft and height is lost on the last part of the run in, just before dropping. It is usual [. . .] to time groups of aircraft, three or four according to the composition of the military units carried, to arrive closely grouped at the dropping zone allowing for slight errors in course to prevent collision risks due to errors in timing. (It may be noted that aircraft 10 seconds apart in time are 600 yards apart (in distance).)

For night attacks the training of pilots in low map reading and country recognition must be as in paragraph 2 above. The importance of having a complete mental picture of the approach run is even greater owing to the difficulty of recognizing features until quite close when flying by moon-light or in poor visibility. In this connection it is usual to train pilots and observes by means of very accurate landscape models from which an accurate impression of the country near the objective can be gained, and to make them learn to draw free-hand without reference to the models or maps, a map of the country covered by the approach, so as to impress the significant features on their memories. Suitable vertical and oblique air photographs are also great value.

The task of navigation falls much more on navigators and second pilots during night approaches, since the captain has to concentrate more upon maintaining the correct height, speed and attitude of the aircraft. Experience has shown that for the main part of the run in, the navigator must have a general view, such as can be obtained from the second Pilot's position or from the upper part of a Whitley turret, and that only for the last final judging of the time to switch on the Red and Green light signals to the paratroops, can the bomb-aimers' panel be used.

4. It is considered that, apart from period flying and formation flying, the air training for paratroop dropping may be carried out in five stages, as follows:—

   (i) Low flying Cross Countries of 45–60 minutes' duration with turning points over selected pinpoints. Six of these flights would be sufficient per crew.

   (ii) The dropping of dummy paratroops in a selected field near the aerodrome for convenience of collecting dummies. Four practices dropping dummies, 8 each time, would be necessary. Upwind, Downwind and Crosswind drops should all be practised.

   (iii) Dusk or moonlight Cross Countries of 46–60 minutes' duration dropping dummies in selected fields. At least two of these Cross Countries would be necessary.

(iv) Low flying Cross Countries of 45–60 minutes' duration with definite times at certain turning points and also a definite time to drop dummies at a selected point about half way round the Cross Country using Photographs for the selection of the dropping field. Two of these flights would be necessary.

(v) One Day and Moonlight rehearsal in co-operation with the other Services, actually dropping the troops and containers. If considered desirable, only the containers need the dropped on the moonlight rehearsal.

5. In addition to the above flying and navigational training for paratroop dropping, it is essential that captains and, in less degree, other members of air crews should be familiar with all the equipment used in the aircraft for paratroop dropping, i.e. method of loading containers in bomb cells, selection of switches, automatic container release switch, fitting of paratroop strop panels and fixing of strops to strong points, and method of closing and opening door of hole.

They should know the general drill for paratroops during:—

(a) Take off.

(b) Cruising

(c) On receiving "Action Stations"

(d) On preparing to drop.

(e) Timing of Red and green Signals.

NOTE. Interval of 5 to 15 seconds from Red to Green and position of Green depending on wind at dropping zone.

(f) Checking whether containers have gone, and if not, dropping on second run.

(g) Recovery procedure with parachute troops aboard, e.g. crash drill abandon aircraft, ditching drill, etc.

6. Finally air crews should be familiar with the procedure at base aerodromes both in preparation for a parachute operation and on the day, including the division of responsibilities between the Air Force and the Army, and the use of Loading manifest forms.

7. During training the value and importance of full liaison and complete understanding between Army and R.A.F. during parachute operations should be emphasized whenever possible.

(sgd.) N. Norman, Group Captain, Commanding,

No. 38 Wing, Royal Air Force.

Parachute dispersal was one of the central challenges of airborne warfare. Although theoretically vertical deployment offered the appearance of precision, the reality was very different. For a start, terrain conditions could mean that paratroopers had to be dropped considerable distance away from their primary objective anyway. When British and Polish paratroopers and glider-borne troops were deployed near Arnhem on 17 September 1944, for example, the fields in which they touched down were actually 7–8 miles (11–13km) from their primary objective. Crossing that distance gave away much of the surprise on which they relied, plus provided the Germans with a window of opportunity to reinforce its defence. But even putting men down in the intended location was a challenge. When the 505th Parachute Infantry Regiment (PIR), part of the 82nd Airborne Division, was dropped over Normandy during the early hours of 6 June 1944, such was the level of its dispersal that the troops were between 6 and 15 miles (10 and 24km) from their DZs. The list of factors that caused dispersal seemed endless: navigation problems, poor visibility, strong winds, anti-aircraft fire, errors in planning, problems when exiting the aircraft, and so on. The text that follows, from the British *Parachute Training Manual*, therefore squarely addresses the technicalities of accurate parachute deployment under combat conditions, bringing a measure of science to the unpredictabilities.

Parachute Training Manual (1944)
TECHNIQUE OF DROPPING
General Principles

24. Although a pilot at a Parachute Training School carries out much repetition flying, this does not mean that the flying lacks interest. On the contrary, the technique of dropping paratroops is a subject of considerable interest because so many factors not met with in normal flying and bombing are involved. Knowledge and judgment will in time enable a pilot to drop his troops at a known landing ground with an accuracy which a new pilot cannot attain. And this skill can only be acquired by experience and application. It can be compared with the art of the old boatman who knows the currents on a particular stretch of water so well that he can, without effort, steer his boat to the spot he desires. The dropping of paratroops can properly be termed an art because the pilot who shows a special interest, or possesses a special aptitude, excels over the pilot who does not.

25. The aim when dropping paratroops is for the paratroop to jump so that he lands on a predetermined spot. An actual spot is not practicable, but a circle with a radius of 50 yards should be aimed at, and with skill, may be achieved. Success can be attained only if both the pilot and the paratroop act correctly; therefore, co-operation and mutual understanding between the pilot and paratroop is essential. Given this basis, the difficulties of accurate dropping are still great, as compared with bombing, for a variety of reasons which are discussed under five headings below.

The Problem of Accurate Flying.

26. This problem can be explained most easily by a simple example. Assume a pilot wishes to drop a paratroop on a particular spot when flying straight into a 15 m.p.h. wind at 500 ft. The amount of drift of a parachute descending at 18 ft. per second is shown by the table (Table I in para. 30) as 183 yards. The pilot therefore should approach the chosen landing spot in a straight line dead into wind. When he has left the spot 183 yards behind (ignoring for the moment all other factors) he should release his paratroop. The difficulties in this case are for the pilot–

  (i) to know when he is exactly over the landing spot;

  (ii) to fly a straight course into wind for 183 yards thereafter (in practice for the reasons stated in paras. 27 and 28 later he will not have to fly as far as 183 yards);

  (iii) to maintain accuracy of height whilst flying this course.

  (iv) to maintain a constant air speed.

With most aircraft, there will be a tendency, as a stick of paratroops leaves, for the aircraft to become nose heavy and for the air speed to increase. This tendency must be guarded against by the pilot. [. . .] The results can be disastrous for the last men and serious for the operational efficiency of the others.

The Problem of Signal Delay.

27. The normal method by which a pilot gives the signal to jump is by pressing an electric switch which shows a green light in the cabin of the aircraft, on seeing which the Despatcher gives the order to the first paratroop to jump. This sequence obviously involves a time lag from the moment the pilot has made up his mind that he has reached the spot required, to the moment the paratroop actually leaves the aircraft. Three human brains and physical reactions are involved, and a time lag of one or more seconds may occur. For this lag again the pilot must make allowance, though it is difficult to predict the correct amount unless the pilot knows his passengers and their time reactions.

The diagram at fig. 33 shows a drop in conditions of no wind. The aircraft pilot made up his mind that he was at the right spot when he was nearly over it at A but by the time he had pressed the switch and the first paratroop had left at "B," there was a delay of 3 seconds during which time the aircraft covered 150 yards (*see* Table II). To this has to be added the throw forward of the paratroop on leaving (perhaps 90 yards) and a slow stick, with the result that the last jumper finds himself landed outside the intended dropping area.

The Problem of Point of Departure.

28. The drift table (Table I in para. 30) assumes that the paratroop jumps from a stationary object at a known height and that his parachute is fully open at that height. In actual fact, he jumps from a moving aircraft the height above the ground may not be precisely known, and the parachute is not fully developed for a period of 2–3 seconds after jumping. During this delay the paratroop has fallen about 100 ft., and he has been carried forward as a result of his jump and the speed (120 m.p.h.) of the aircraft from which he jumped, for about 90 yards. It will be seen, therefore, how many factors under this heading alone exist to upset the pilot's calculations.

The diagram (fig. 34) illustrates how an aircraft dropping in a slight following wind, has failed to make allowance for the throw forward and wind, with the result that the last paratroop is landed beyond the spot intended.

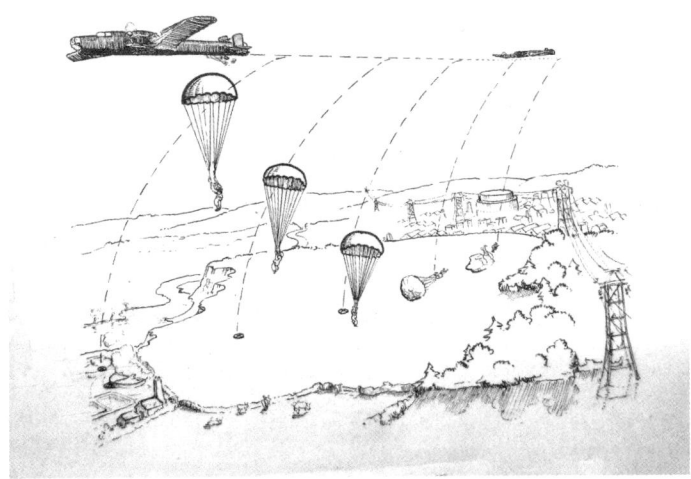

Fig. 34. Point of departure.

The Problem of Rate of Descent.

29. This is one of the greatest difficulties because it will be affected by up and down currents of air, by the performance and shape of the parachute, by the weight of the parachute, and by other unpredictable factors. Up and down currents are caused both by turbulence and wind, and they will vary from day to day and from hour to hour. In time, the experienced pilot at a school will learn, after dropping his first stick, what the effect of such currents is likely to be at any particular time and day, and adapt his dropping technique accordingly. In certain atmospheric conditions, however, it will be difficult to make accurate allowance for such currents. Such conditions are particularly prevalent in tropical countries where it may happen that the first jumper of a stick is supported sufficiently long by an up current for him to land after the last jumper in the stick.

Oscillation or delayed development of the parachute will also affect its rate of descent and these factors will be impossible to predict accurately. The effect of the weight of a paratroop on rate of descent is discussed in Chapter III, para. 49, but this is not of great account if the jump is made from a low height.

The diagram (fig. 35) shows various factors which can affect the rate and direction of descent of paratroops as follows :—

No. 1.	Oscillation.
No. 2.	Gusts
No. 3.	Delayed opening.
No. 4.	Normal descent.
No. 5.	Air currents off hillside.

Fig. 35. Rate of descent.

The Problem of Drift.

30. The drift table at Table I indicates the position at which a 28-ft. parachute will land if it floats down at varying known rates of descent from a stationary object (such as the top of a tower), and if both the rate of, descent and the drift are constant. Unfortunately none of these factors are constant, and therefore the drift table must be taken merely as a general guide to what is likely to happen, and not as a guide to what will in fact happen. The drift will be affected by variations in the strength and directions of the wind between the aircraft and the ground. Whilst it is impossible in practice for a pilot to prejudge these variations at an unknown D.Z., he should in time gain considerable knowledge of them at his own school dropping ground. If available, a rear gunner can usually provide the most accurate estimation of drift.

The diagram at fig. 36 indicates how a pilot, dropping across wind has failed to allow enough for drift.

Fig. 36. Drift.

TABLE I. Table of Variation in Drift for Different Dropping Heights, Wind Speeds and Rates of Descent

HEIGHT OF DROP Rates of Descent in Feet per Second	Wind Speed 5 m.p.h.			Wind Speed 10 m.p.h.			Wind Speed 15 m.p.h.			Wind Speed 20 m.ph		
	16	18	20	16	18	20	16	18	20	16	18	20
300 ft...	38.3	34.0	30.6	76.6	68.0	61.2	114.8	102.1	91.9	153.1	136.0	122.5
400 ft. ..	53.6	47.6	42.9	107.2	95.3	85.7	160.7	142.9	128.6	214.4	190.4	171.5
500 ft. ..	68.9	61.2	55.1	137.8	122.5	110.2	206.6	183.7	165.4	275.6	244.8	220.5
600 ft. ..	84.2	74.9	67.4	168.5	149.7	134.7	252.5	224.5	202.1	336.9	299.2	269.5
700 ft. ..	99.5	88.5	79.6	199.1	176.9	159.2	298.4	265.3	238.9	398.1	353.6	318.5
800 ft. ..	114.8	102.1	91.9	229.7	204.1	183.7	344.3	306.1	275.6	459.4	408.0	367.5
900 ft. ..	130.1	115.7	104.1	260.3	231.4	208.2	390.2	346.9	312.4	520.6	462.4	416.5
1,000 ft.	145.4	129.3	116.4	291.0	258.6	232.7	436.1	387.8	349.1	581.9	516.8	465.5

$$D = 0.49 \frac{W}{V} (H-50)$$

D = Drift in yards.   V= = Rate of Descent–per/sec.

W = Wind Speed–m.p.h. H = Dropping Height–in feet.

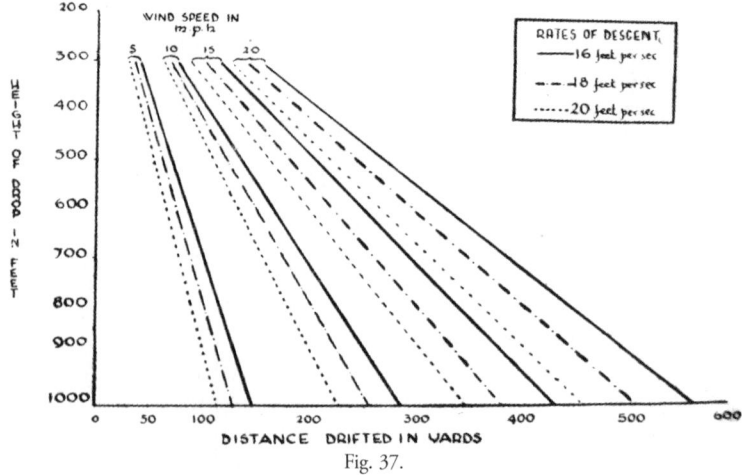

Fig. 37.

TABLE II. Distance covered per second by an aircraft at a given air-speed and wind-speed.

Flying Up Wind

AirSpeed (m.p.h.)	Wind Speed (m.p.h.)	Ground Speed (m.p.h.)	Distance covered per secondyards.
90	15	75	36.6
90	10	80	39.1
90	5	85	41.5
100	15	85	41.5
100	10	90	44.0
100	5	95	46.5
110	15	95	46.5
110	10	100	49.0
110	5	105	51.3
120	15	105	51.3
120	10	110	54.0
120	5	115	56.2

Flying In Calm

90	Nil	90	44.0
100	Nil	100	49.0
110	Nil	110	54.0
120	Nil	120	58.7

Flying Down Wind

AirSpeed (m.p.h.)	Wind Speed (m.p.h.)	Ground Speed (m.p.h.)	Distance covered per secondyards.
90	5	95	46.5
90	10	100	49.0
90	15	105	51.3
100	5	105	51.3
100	10	110	54.0
100	15	115	56.2
110	5	115	56.2
110	10	120	58.7
110	15	125	61.1
120	5	125	61.1
120	10	130	63.5
120	15	135	66.0

Stick Dropping

31. The principles governing the dropping of sticks do not vary in any way from those governing the dropping of individuals. The success of putting down a stick accurately will depend almost entirely on whether the first man is dropped correctly. In stick dropping, however, the effect of wind direction and strength assumes greater importance than with single drops, and the difficulties of accurate flying are increased by the effect on trim which the dropping of 10 or more men may involve. As the paratroops leave the aircraft, it will normally become nose heavy thus tending to increase the airspeed and cause a loss of height which must at all costs be avoided. Steep turns before the dropping run must also be avoided and particularly excess speed. One of the best ways to lose excess speed if it can be done without affecting the jumper or deployment of the parachute, is to lower the flaps or undercarriage, or both.

It is preferable to fly either into wind or across wind when dropping paratroops. With stick dropping, down-wind flying should always be avoided, otherwise the length of the stick on the ground will be greatly increased. A simple example will illustrate this point. Assume that a stick of 10 has to be dropped and that it will take

10 seconds for them to leave the aircraft which will fly at 110 m.p.h. with a wind of 15 m.p.h. The graph at fig. 37 shows that if flying into wind, the ground distance covered by the aircraft during the stick exit – which will be the length of the stick on the ground – is 465 yards, whilst if flying down wind the length is 611 yards.

From the point of view of the pilot, a beam wind is probably the easiest as he only has to calculate and allow for drift at 90° to his track.

Dropping sticks in wind directions which are not either into wind or across wind involves risks which should not be taken unless the dropping area is large, the wind strength is slight, or the pilot very experienced.

32. When dropping into wind it is a safe and simple rule to put on the red light to stop jumping when the end of the dropping area is reached. But when dropping down wind the last paratroop must leave at a distance before the end of the dropping area greater than the length of his drift. This is due to the invariable time lag in communication between the pilot and the paratroop and the initial forward fall of the paratroop. Thus in calm, beam, or down-wind conditions, it is advisable for the pilot to put on the stop light for jumping before the last safe spot is actually reached.

It is useful for pilots to set a stop watch or count at 1 second intervals during team exits so that they may know when the last man of their stick ought to have left the aircraft: alternatively, at a school, the Despatcher can indicate to the pilot by switching a light in the cockpit or by inter com.

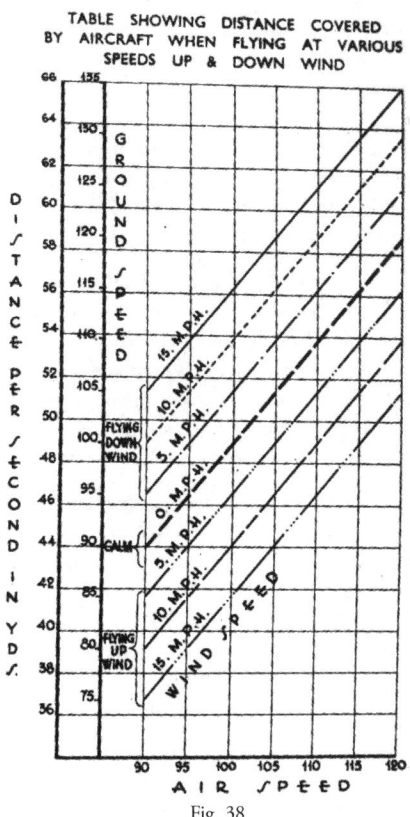

Fig. 38.

Formation Dropping

33. This is a requirement of school training because it gives paratroops company training on the ground after landing. This is necessary since on daylight operations, it may well prove essential to put a large number of paratroops onto the ground in a very short space of time if they are to be capable of effective action. This can only be done by formation flying. The principles governing formation dropping are similar to those already set out but greater responsibility rests on the leading aircraft which will normally control the dropping.

There are two main types of formation that can be used – line astern and Vic – and their use is governed entirely by the requirements of the drop.

34. *Line astern formation* is particularly suitable in long, narrow dropping areas, and where the number of aircraft is not too great. It allows for great manoeuvrability on the part of the aircraft, but interference from slip stream may affect the following aircraft so that they will have to "step-up" or "step-down" according to the type of aircraft. If they have to "step up," the last aircraft may find itself so high that accurate dropping is difficult, or alternatively, "stepping-down" may not allow the rear aircraft sufficient dropping height. In practice, it is best to avoid "stepping-up" or "down" if the slip-stream difficulties can be overcome. In this kind of formation, each pilot has the opportunity to use his own judgment for releasing his paratroops.

35. *Vic formation* in flights of three or five aircraft allows for greater concentration of aircraft over the dropping area in a given space of time, combined with more compact patterns on the ground. This formation is not so manoeuvrable as Line Astern and is difficult for reducing speed; therefore, correct adherence to the line of approach and a steady air speed on the approach are essential, and a correspondingly greater responsibility rests on the Leader. Close formations of five aircraft in Vic formation are in advisable, except for demonstration purpose sat a known dropping ground.

36. To obtain concentration of paratroops on the ground in an exercise or on operations, Squadron Vic formation of three aircraft is probably the best procedure. Providing the leader of the Vic drops accurately, the pilots on his flanks may be comparatively inexperienced, for they can release their paratroops simultaneously with their leader, either by visual timing or under R/T instructions. So long as they are in good formation, the ultimate pattern on the ground will be compact.

Exercise Dropping

37. The final application of dropping technique arrives when a team and containers have to be landed after a cross-country flight at an unfamiliar dropping zone. To his dropping skill the pilot must add the expert use and appreciation of large scale maps (1 in. to 1 mile) and mosaic photographs. If possible the selected area must be photographed by a vertical air camera and the area compared and transferred to the large scale map. From this map the height above sea level of the area may be determined. Several considerations affect the "run-in," perhaps the foremost being the shape of the area; obstructions, wind speed and direction are also vital factors. The selected track of the stick is eventually plotted on the 1-in. map, and the line extended to form a "line of approach" of about 5 miles in length and preferably terminating at some easily recognisable pin-point. This pin-point is then co-ordinated to the smaller scale map, and its track and distance measured. Normal cross-country navigation is employed to reach this pin-point, after which the aircraft is headed on the run-in to the dropping area. Wind speed and direction will have been previously estimated, but must be carefully checked so that a course may be set to make good the track of the run-in. Height and air speed are reduced; close and accurate map-reading, together with timing, are then essential in order to bring the

aircraft precisely over the correct and pre-determined point on the boundary of the field where dropping is to be carried out. It is not possible, especially in formation, to make last moment alterations of course, but, provided the line of approach is made absolutely accurate some way from the D.Z., the aircraft should arrive at the correct point of the dropping area at the proper height, airspeed and time, and drop the "stick" on the first run across. In any case, it is usually better to drop on an incorrect area the first time than circle trying to find the exact location.

Night Dropping

38. The technique of dropping by night is similar to that already described for day flying.

When dropping at D.Zs. other than a school dropping ground, low-flying cross-country navigation will be more difficult than by day and it will be essential to carry a navigator. He must assume full responsibility for the run up and dropping signals, as the pilot will be occupied with his flying, and in particular, in ensuring that he is not flying too fast at the moment of jumping. There will in any case be a tendency to fly too fast at night which will be accentuated by the need to lose height which will usually be necessary just before the drop.

There will be greater difficulty in judging the correct duration of the green light and the moment at which to switch on the "stop" signal, particularly on dark nights when obstructions are hardly discernible. If several aircraft are dropping over the same D.Z. they should fly at different heights.

Wind direction and strength are more difficult to assess by night than by day. But wind strength and air currents are likely to be less at night, which will assist accuracy in dropping.

Water Dropping

39. Dropping into water is very similar to dropping on to land. Movement of the surface of the water will afford a guide to wind speed and direction, but this will be difficult to assess unless the wind is fairly high.

For training purposes a boat can be stationed in the middle of the area and if it can ride at anchor, it will form a good wind indicator. It is inadvisable to use a smoke indicator, as in light airs the smoke will tend to lie on the surface, and so hinder the work of rescue craft.

The continuity of the dropping is dependant upon the speed at which the paratroops are picked up by the rescue launch, which in turn is governed by the accuracy with which the pilot drops. It is helpful to the pilot, if after reaching a parachute, the launch will retain its position relative to the marker boat, in order that the pilot may later gauge the drift for his next drop.

40. The depth of the water is important as paratroops must not be dropped into shallow water which may be present round the edges of a lake, nor into water

which contains obstructions. In these circumstances markers may be necessary and additional care exercised by the pilot. Providing rescue facilities are adequate, there to need be no limit as the number dropped in a "stick."

Dropping into water at night without aids is not difficult if there is moonlight as this defines the water area clearly.

4. METHODS OF DROPPING

41. Various systems that can be employed for dropping paratroops are as follows:—

    (i) Judgment by air crew.

    (ii) Judgment by paratroop section leader

   (iii) Ground markings.

   (iv) Paratroop sight.

    (v) Radio.

Each method is briefly discussed below.

Judgement by Air Crew

42. At a school, if this method is adopted, the pilot will probably have to rely on his own judgment alone, assisted perhaps by ground markings, and he will be responsible for operating the signals which control the jumping. If a full air crew is carried the bomb-aimer navigator will be given the responsibility of controlling the run up and the dropping of signals.

43. The most useful aid to a pilot dropping by judgement is a smoke indicator in the form of a candle or generator let into the ground in the centre of the dropping area. Such an aid is closely related to natural conditions, and is valuable telling the pilot the strength and direction of the wind on the ground. It is the aid most generally useful as it may well be possible to use smoke at or near an operational dropping ground.

At known dropping ground, such as is used by a school, it is normally satisfactory to allow pilots to drop by judgement alone, unless strong or erratic winds are blowing. But if this method is adopted for exercises, experienced pilots should be used, and it is incumbent on them to make themselves fully acquainted with the D.Z. and the weather conditions at the spot before taking off. D.Zs vary greatly in difficulty and they should be selected for advanced training according to the standard of the pilot.

If the weather conditions on any particular day are expected to be difficult, it is helpful to drop a dummy before live jumps start.

The previous section has indicated difficulties connected with dropping by judgment alone. Fortunately these are not, in practice, as great as might be expected, unless dropping takes place from a considerable height, because some of the problems will cancel out each other.

44. The following are useful rules for air crews:—

(*a*) Always start an accurate run-up at least one mile from the dropping ground. In the case of D.Zs the run up must be much longer.

(*b*) During the run-up and dropping never skid or make any other sudden alteration in the course of the aircraft.

(*c*) Continue straight flight some distance after the dropping ground.

(*d*) If not formating, never follow too closely in the wake of an aircraft in front.

(*e*) Jumping nearly always starts too late rather than too early.

(*f*) A pilot should always, if circumstances permit, look at the result of his drops, and if the paratroops have not landed where he intended, find out the reason why.

(*g*) A pilot should always know the standard of the paratroops he is carrying.

45. Interest in the standard of dropping can be increased by a system of marks awarded to pilots for accuracy of dropping. This can conveniently be carried out at a school when the trainees are dropping in pairs. An area is marked on the ground within which the first of each pair should land, marks being awarded according to the distance from the centre of the circle that the landing is made.

A record should always be kept of inaccurate dropping so that unreliable pilots can be identified and if necessary removed.

Judgment by Paratroop Section Leader

46. This system is employed occasionally on aircraft using a door exit (*e.g.*, C.47). The leader of the paratroop section is known as the jump-master. During careful briefing of the pilot and jump-master—usually with the assistance of aerial photographs of the dropping zone— a pin-point is selected from which the pilot is to make his run-up to the dropping zone; the direction of the run-up is settled, and the jump-master, having due regard to wind conditions, selects some landmark opposite the door of the aircraft at which he will commence dropping his stick. When the pilot arrives at the selected pin-point he switches a signal light and the jump-master (No. 1) stands at the door; looking out. When he sees the selected landmark opposite to him, he jumps and the rest of the stick follows him. In this case the responsibility for the placing of the stick rests with the jump-master and not with the pilot or observer.

Ground Markings

47. The employment of ground markings useful at a busy school as it assists accurate dropping by all aircraft. A satisfactory system of ground signals is as follows:

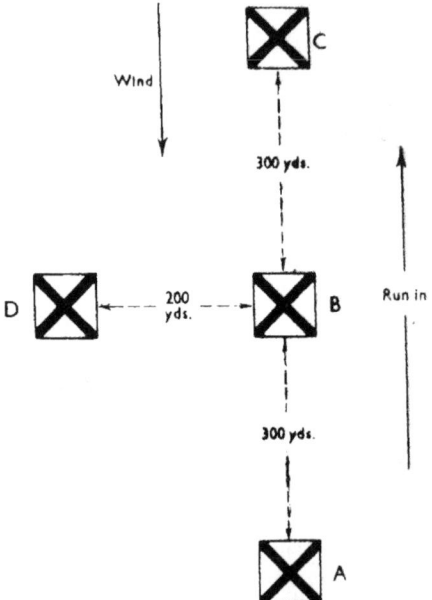

Markers   20 feet square — Yellow with Black Cross.
Line of Flight — over markers A, B, C.
Signal to Drop is given when pilot is level with the markers B, D.

Fig. 39.

A smoke indicator in the centre of the dropping ground is an added convenience to indicate the strength and direction of the wind at ground level.

48. The Officer in charge of the dropping area is responsible for laying out the ground signals and in doing this he is guided by exactly the same principles as those governing the pilot who is dropping by judgment. It is desirable for the chief pilot at least to be in wireless communication with the officer in charge of the dropping area so that the position of the ground markings can be altered if necessary. Good co-operation between them can result in great accuracy when dropping large numbers of troops.

Additional ground signals and means of communication between the aircraft and officer in charge of the dropping ground are explained in Chapter VI.

The use of ground markings is apt to make pilots slack in their appreciation of the problems of dropping, and this fact must be watched at a school where the use of such markings may be desirable owing to employment of inexperienced pilots or to large output. It is also necessary to have a clearly defined responsibility for laying out the ground signals and for changing them if they are found to be incorrectly placed.

The *Glider Manual* was issued by the RAF's No. 1 Glider Training School in April 1942. The Training School had been located at RAF Ringway, but it was relocated to RAF Thame (today Haddenham Airfield in Buckinghamshire) in December 1941, Thame also coming to be home of the No. 2 Glider Training School. The excerpt from the manual here explains some of the key considerations for a successful glider combat operation.

Glider Manual (1942)

Method of Attack.

68. The order of operations for an airborne attack might be on the following lines:—

(a) Air Reconnaissance.

(b) Bombing of enemy fighter aerodromes, and of R.D.F. stations as a vital part of fighter defence, perhaps over several days.

(c) Intensified bombing as above, on the night preceding the attack.

(d) Vigorous dive-bombing at dawn on ground defences, in successive waves, to disclose the small-arms defences of the area.

(e) Ground-strafing by waves of fighters on the defences disclosed;

(f) Lending of parachute troops shortly after the above, possibly accompanied by gliders, with fighter screen, and with standing patrols of dive-bombers and fighters ready to support ground troops when signalled for assistance. These landings might begin before the bombing attack ended, whilst it was lifted in the immediate landing areas only.

(g) Glider-borne troops arrive shortly after parachute troops, who have prepared the ground. Fighter cover continues.

(h) Troop-carrying aeroplanes might land on prepared ground.

(i) Large scale sabotage and diversion operations might be carried out simultaneously.

(j) Land support (or evacuation) follows.

Light and Weather.

69. The need for good weather is a serious limitation to glider-borne operations. The weather must be such as to give good serviceability of aerodromes, favourable wind direction for the journey, moderate wind strength if parachutes are to be used, and good visibility at least for lending. If a large formation is to be launched to arrive simultaneously, visibility must be good, but small successive waves might make use of bad visibility and cloud cover in which a large formation would involve undue risk of collision. Vulnerability in the air would be much reduced. But bad visibility near the ground (mist or fog) would make landing extremely difficult, and the full use of cloud cover depends on the successful development of blind towing.

70. The great advantages of launching an attack by daylight are obvious, e.g., preliminary assembly, emplaning, take-off, assembly at rendezvous and accurate navigation are simplified.

But an airborne attack carried out wholly in daylight against a well defended area could be very costly.

70 A. If the landing is to be at dusk or shortly after nightfall, weather forecasts can be relied on to a much greater extent than for a dawn landing. Reconnaissance aircraft may have been able to obtain up-to-date information for an evening landing, but the weather may change considerably overnight before a dawn landing. The evening landing also allows enemy fighters to be grounded during the attack as a result of intensive fighter and bomber sweeps during the day.

71. Landing at dusk has all the advantages and disadvantages of full daylight take-off and approach. To land in exactly the right light, in reasonable visibility without too great a delay before advantage can be taken of darkness, requires very careful timing. The smaller the force, the simpler this task. The airborne force, knowing its tasks exactly and having some hours of darkness to assemble and concentrate to, has a distinct advantage over the enemy. The latter cannot be certain of the objective, and must collect and handle reserves in the dark. Above all, the attackers are largely immune from air attack. The disadvantage to the attackers of having to move in the dark is by no means a serious one to well-trained troops who have studied the ground intimately from maps, air photographs and models. The half hour or more of twilight which is available after landing affords a good opportunity to get the lie of the land and to start concentrating.

72. To land early in the night just after it gets dark gives the advantages of a daylight take-off, and the attackers still have some hours of darkness at their disposal. But glider-borne attack by night has not yet been proved feasible, and in addition to being risky as regards the actual landing, depends on the successful development of night towing. The take-off might be organised in good moonlight conditions, assembly in the air being assisted by signal lights or wireless from the air or from the ground. But a landing even in moonlight might result in high casualties. Flares could hardly be used for landing in a surprise operation. A dawn landing is more likely. A preceding force of parachutists might however be put down at night, night dropping is highly developed.

73. The advantages in approaching and landing at night are as follow:

(a) No fighter escorts are required.

(b) Aimed Flak can be largely avoided.

(c) The enemy is unable to locate the landing areas immediately.

The main disadvantages of a night take-off and landing are:—

(a) The added complication of night assembly take-off.

(b) A greatly decreased rate of take-off and landing and the impossibility of flying in formation so that the force arrives in driblets.

(c) The difficulty of accurate navigation by night. Even prominent landmarks, such as water, white cliffs and isolated woods can only be seen clear conditions and bright moonlight. Searchlights, gun flashes and bright fires greeting increase the difficulty of seeing ground at night.

74. Landings at dawn entail the same disadvantages given (a) to (b) above. Very accurate timing is essential; the enemy are very much in the alert from first light if airborne attack is at all likely; as the light grows, the landings are liable to air attack which may seriously interfere with assembly and concentration. Accurate navigation may still be difficult at dawn owing to ground mist; flak although not so accurate as in full daylight will be more effective than at night. However, the attackers can see what they are doing: confusion is less likely and the objectives should be more speedily reached.

Assembly and Take-off.

75. Success or failure in most operations of war depends very much on correct timing, and exact adherence to that timing. Especially is this so with Airborne Forces, which co-operate intimately with the R.A.F. and in fact, depend on it for transport. The hour at which a unit sub-unit is time to pass a point, reach an assembly area or aerodrome, and emplane, is worked out to ensure exact co-ordination of the operation as a whole. A Commander who fails to function up to time may jeopardise not only the lives of those under his command but the success of the whole operation.

76. It has been held that the collection of gliders on aerodromes for a major operation would be so conspicuous as to offer an easy target for bombing, especially as it might be necessary to stand by for favourable weather, But this need not be so if the girdlers are dispersed over several aerodromes, as they must be if a large force is to take off within a reasonable time. The force might assemble in peace at far rearward aerodromes, and on the day previous to the operation, given a good weather forecast, be towed to a forward base where aircraft would be marshaled (perhaps at night) for take-off at dawn. This procedure was followed by the enemy in the invasion of Crete.

77. The length of time between the first landing at the objective and complete assembly as an organised force is of first importance. The speed with which the whole force can be put into the air therefore is a vital factor, since the total landing time will depend on the total take-off time. A further reason for shortening the take-off time is that troops going into action should not be kept seated in aircraft too long. The total lending time can be roughly estimated by picturing the formation in the air, and dividing its length by its ground speed. Appreciation of the Importance of short trial take-off time no doubt accounts for the very long runways which the Germans have built at many aerodromes, which allow for the marshalling of large numbers of gliders in addition to the actual take-off run. The runway at Stavanger is already over 2,000 yards long and has boon double in width. Runway aerodromes seem essential for any large scale operation.

78. On such a runway, given well-trained ground crews, twenty 25-seater gliders, arranged in order of priority, of take-off as on an aircraft carrier, might assemble in 600 yards, with their tugs, leaving over 1200 yards for the actual take-off run. With

reasonably good organisation and freedom from mishaps, all the aircraft might take off within twenty minutes. Thirty such aerodromes could deal with a fleet of 600 to 800 gliders carrying an airborne force of 10,000 men and their equipment. For reasons of navigation and protection, such a fleet would probably proceed in mass formations. Prompt assembly in the air is therefore important. If the take-off were before first light, aircraft with tail lights might follow one another to the air rendezvous where the whole fleet would converge. Alternatively, the fleet might proceed in a series of waves. Beacon lights might be set within friendly territory to absorb initial errors of timing. Radio homing devices might be used, being either dropped by parachute from an aeroplane on to the objective or nearby, giving automatic signals, or being operated by agents in or near the landing area. on at the release point.

Methods of Towing and Approach.

79. Three methods of towing and approach seem to be offered:—

(a) Towing to the required height to allow release long distance from the landing area.

   This method has the advantages of likelier surprise and earlier release of the tug for further duty; the tug does not come within range of ground or air defences near the objective; the period of tow, during which both aircraft are more vulnerable, is shortened.

   From the point of release, the gliders should be within sight of one another. Experienced navigators would load the way, perhaps in powered aircraft. The risk of collision between gliders of similar flying characteristics would be negligible. The maximum error in E.T.A. should not exceed five minutes either way. On nearing the objective, height would be lost as rapidly as possible in order to shorten the period passed within range of ground defences.

   The disadvantages of releasing a long distance from the objective are:— good visibility is required, which aids the defences; greater responsibility is placed on the glider pilot, who probably casts off out of sight of the general landing area and must navigate under more difficult conditions than the navigator of a multi-seater tug. (To carry an additional navigator in each glider would reduce the numbers available for skilled military tasks on landing.) Once released from tow, the glider cannot outclimb bad weather, or make long de tours to avoid it.

(b) Towing, possibly above or in cloud cover, to a release point from which the general landing area can be identified.

   This method greatly simplifies the duties of the glider pilot, but involves greater risk for the tug, a longer vulnerable period on tow, and possible loss of surprise. It would be risky if attempted against any considerable fighter opposition.

(c) Towing at low altitude to the immediate vicinity of the landing ground, to obtain surprise for at least a part of the force, and to make R.D.F. detection and A.A. and fighter attack more difficult. This method demands accurate judgment of the moment for the Germans on the Continent, provided the objective within the range of our fighter escorts and allows of the areas of heavy Flak, airborne attack is certainly possible in daylight without sustaining heavy casualties. But to reach an objective well inland and beyond our effective fighter range would be a hazardous operation

92. The guns of bomber tugs could defend a formation but such guns as could be mounted on the gliders themselves could hardly be formidable against fighters, It seems inevitable that a glider formation on tow must operate by night, in cloud cover, or with a strong "fighter umbrella". Fighters, if used as tugs, would be available for defence after the release.

93. Enemy fighters attacking a glider formation would themselves be highly vulnerable to attack by defending fighters, since the former must be flown comparatively slowly to attack effectively, and their manoeuvres should not be difficult to foresee. Defence by a fighter screen would force any attacking fighters to fly at higher speeds then are suitable for attacking gliders, or to deal with the defending fighters first.

Loss of Range.

94. A free glider should be able to take reasonable evasive action against a single fighter, although it would be difficult to cope with two simultaneously. But evasive action is limited in time, owing to the extra loss of height, especially if the flaps are used. On trials the loss of range during continuous evasive action by a free glider has been between 25% and 40%. If the glider could be forced to land short of the objective, the purpose of the attack would have been achieved. Ample height margin is therefore needed if air attack is considered at all likely.

Landing.

95. An airborne striking force must be highly concentrated in time and space. If a single aerodrome did not offer sufficient capacity, the extension of the landing area by the use of fields would be necessary, and would greatly reduce the total landing time. Probably no more than 3,000 troops per hour could be put down on an aerodrome. Few fields are so obstructed as to make glider landings impossible, if damage to the glider is accepted providing the crew are uninjured, and especially if parachute troops have prepared the ground. The gliders themselves must be looked upon as "expendable" stores in the majority of operations in which they will be used, although this is very far from the truth in the case of pilots and crews.

96. Glider pilots might not all land at specific points in a surprise mass attack; large zones could be indicated in which the majority could land according to

the conditions met. Pilots might be instructed to land in groups of about 7 or 10 aircraft. They would be familiarised with the main features by means of air-photographs and models. In the selection of the correct tactical lending point, the gilder pilot might require the assistance of the commander of the troops in the glider, who must be fully proficient in map-reading from aircraft. The troops should be able to fulfil their military rules from whatever starting point within the area the pilot was able to select, probably acting as independent units until an advanced stage of the battle.

97. Although the ground defences may have been forced to reveal their positions by dive-bombing, and put out of action before the landing of the airborne force, the enemy must be considered intelligent enough, if he suspects the intention, to order a proportion of the ground defences to hold their fire, or to make use of dummies and of mobile defences constantly changed.

98. The glider pilot should mistrust large and apparently unobstructed fields occurring within a generally obstructed area. If the enemy considers airborne attack likely, he will hardly have overlooked the opportunity of trapping the attacking force by leaving a few areas without visible obstructions, which would prove on landing either to have hidden obstructions or to be covered by machine guns, or even armoured vehicles, which last could be deadly to an airborne force directly after landing.

99. If good cover existed on the margin of the landing area, the pilot might well aim to end his landing run close to this cover even at some risk of collision with the boundary. If the glider came to rest near the middle of a field, the Crew would be exposed on all sides whilst deplaning and assembling, and the glider would form an obstruction to the landing area.

100. But gliders would not normally be landed within range of immediate opposition. The German glider operations in Crete demonstrated that landings amongst highly organized defences are very costly.

101. If the general landing area were foreseen by the defenders, smoke screens might be laid over it. To land through such a Smoke-screen could be a very risky operation. Conversely, Smoke-screens might be laid by the attacking force to cover their approach, landing and assembly, perhaps incidentally providing a landmark and a wind indicator. A known defence position might be blinded in this way, by laying a smoke screen directly in front of it. Several smoke grenades and candles exist for ground action, and in addition the following three types of smoke may be used to cover landing:—

(a) Smoke ejected from containers carried in aircraft.

By this means a really good smoke curtain can be lain at high speed, and its depth depends only on the number of aircraft used. Three aircraft, flying one above the other and echeloned slightly back from the lowest, can lay a very good continuous curtain 400 feet from ground level. The dancer of this method is the vulnerability of the loading aircraft, but it will appear suddenly an only for a short time. Gliders and parachutists can land unseen behind this curtain.

(b) White phosphorus Bombs. These are very useful for making the end or corners of a required smoke screen as a guide to smoke-laying aircraft.

(c) Ordinary Smoke Candles. These can be dropped large numbers from aircraft to form a smoke screen in very quickly, perhaps to cover the approach of Smoke-laying aircraft. [. . .]

105. In the first phase of an operation which was strongly opposed, there would probably be no assembly beyond groups of company strength. Units must be ready to act independently. Full organisation could only be expected in a later phase of the battle unless opposition were slight. The Crete campaign shows that rapid disorganisation sets in if airborne troops are not prepared for impendent action smell units. An airborne force might be required to operate up to 500 miles from its base aerodromes, in the first instance against moderato resistance consisting of small arms fire, though subsequently it might have to meet attack by armoured fighting vehicles. Even after the assembly of its various units, it must be prepared to be self-contained up to a period of at least three days, and in certain circumstances might be isolated for long periods and might have to depend on airborne supply for its maintenance.

All military operations require exhaustive planning to maximise the possibilities of a victorious or even merely efficient outcome, and airborne operations required an unusually high degree of prior preparation. Airborne operations are often what we refer to as an example of 'combined operations', the coordination of aircraft (both those deploying the paratroopers and those providing supporting escort and ground-attack sorties), airborne infantry and ground forces in one carefully timetabled operation. If a single element of the whole should fall out of sync with the others, the whole enterprise can end in disaster. The following document was issued by the British Army in 1945, and provides a detailed set of guidelines for conducting a major airborne mission. Because of the date of writing, the document's authors have the advantage of bringing together a wealth of prior experience, from small-scale special operations jumps through to the mass deployments of D-Day and elsewhere.

Allied glider reinforcements land in France by glider on D-Day, 6 June 1944.

From *Paratrooper and Glider Operations Standard Procedure* (1945)

PART I – STANDARD OPERATIONAL PROCEDURE FOR AIRBORNE OPERATIONS AND EXERCISES

ORGANISATION

1. A combined Air Force and Army organisation is normally established by the Allied Forces. The preparation for planning and sanctioning of the launching of an airborne operation is the responsibility of the Air Commander-in-Chief in the theatre of operations, who is responsible until the airborne forces reach the ground.

2. The Air Commander is to control the launching of an all airborne force from a Headquarters at which the Army Commander, and the Commanders of all subordinate air formations concerned, are to be represented.

3. Corps Headquarters are established by both British and American airborne formations for the normal exercise of command and control of operations in the field.

4. Air operational control on the same level is effected jointly at a Combined Operational Control Center which is specially set up for each operation.

5. Close liaison is maintained between Corps EQ. and R.A.F. Group H.Q. and U.S.T.C.C at which level detailed plans and arrangements for despatch of an airborne force are made.

[...]

STAFF PROCEDURE

Exercises

9. Army and Air Staff are to arrange details of exercises at a co-ordinating conference, after which the necessary orders and forms are to be completed and issued. [. . .]

Operations

10. Procedure for laying on of operations follows that for exercise, except that staff planning is limited to arranging details necessary to give effect to Commanders' plans. For security reasons representation at Conferences is limited. [. . .]

AIRFIELD PROCEDURE

11. A fixed Command Post, plainly marked, is to be established in each Station Operations Block, at which the Station Commander's representative and the

Airborne Control Section are to be located, and is to be connected by telephone with the troops' billet areas, the leading areas, the Flying Control and the airfield PBX.

12. A report Centre is to be located centrally and clearly marked in each aircraft dispersal area, glider marshaling area, or other such convenient area for the troops. The routes to these centres are to be clearly signposted from the airfield main entrance.

13. Prior to the arrival of the troops, the Station Commander is to give the Airborne Control Officer at least one copy of the aircraft parking diagram showing the numbering and location of aircraft and the sequence of take-off.

14. All aircraft and gliders are to be numbered on both sides of the fuselage in accordance with Form AA or Form AB. Gliders are to be numbered on the port upper side of the tailplane surface in addition.

15. When troops arrive at the airfield in vehicles, wherever possible, they should do so as a complete stick or glider load per vehicle. Each vehicle is to bear the corresponding number (or numbers where any one vehicle is carrying more than one aircraft or glider load) to the aircraft or glider. Numbers are to be marked on the right front mudguard.

16. The Airborne Control Section is to be responsible for troops on arrival on airfields and for the directing of vehicles and troops to report Centres, where they are, if possible, to be met by a number of the aircrew or glider crew.

17. A reserve of aircraft and/or gliders is to be hold and clearly shown on the marking diagram. Priority allocation is to be made by the Airborne Control Officer. The decision as to whether or when reserve aircraft or gliders shall take off is to be made by the R.A.F. Station Commander in the light of the existing air situation.

18. Once Airborne troops have explained and Forms B have been collected, the entire despatching procedure is to be an R.A.F. responsibility.

AIRCREW PROCEDURE

19. The Captain of the tug aircraft is Captain of the glider combination until the moment of release.

LOADING AND INSPECTIONS

[. . .]

Aircrew Duties

21. (a) The Pilot or Bomb Aimer is to accompany the Stick Commander on an inspection of the aircraft as outlined on the aircraft inspection card prior to the

loading of containers onto the aircraft. On completion of this inspection, he is to sign Form B (Parachute).

(b) The Bomb Aimer is to check the correct functioning of the container release mechanism before containers are loaded onto the aircraft.

(c) The Bomb Aimer is to receive detailed information from the Stick Commander as to the time of dropping the containers.

(d) The Pilot or Bomb Aimer is to make a final mechanical and loading check of the aircraft 60 minutes before the time of explaning. He is to immediately advise his C.O. and the Airborne Control Officer if his aircraft is not able to take off on schedule, and is to assist in supervising the transfer of the load to any spare aircraft assigned.

Glider operations

[. . .]

23. Army commanders are to be responsible for preparation of loads, submission of non-standard loads for checking, provision of troughs and lashings, preparation of Forms AB and the appropriate part of form B (Glider), loading of glider (in the presence of glider pilots) and briefing of Air Loading Troops. Troughs, Learnings, etc. may, in certain cases, be stored at R.A.F. airfields as a matter of convenience.

24. R.A.F Station Commanders are to be responsible for preparation of gliders (including fitting or removal of seats as necessary), provision of loading ramps, checking of non-standard loads on request, preparation of the appropriate part of Form B (Gliders), numbering of aircraft and gliders briefing of aircrews and glider pilots and dispatch of aircraft.

25. Airborne Control Sections are to be responsible for guiding and explaining of Air Landing troops, and action on Forms as detailed.

26. If possible glider pilots are to present during loading and are to make a final mechanical and loading check 60 minutes before the time of explaining. If any case of doubt, the tug pilot is to have the final authority. The Senior Glider Passenger is to carry out a final check with the Glider Pilot before explaining and signing Form B (Glider). The Glider Pilot is to sign Form 700 (Aircraft Servicing Form) after his final check before take off.

27. Tug or glider pilots are to advice the R.A.F. Commander and the Airborne Control Officer immediately if the tug aircraft or glider is not able to take off on schedule and the glider pilots are to assist in the transfer of loading to any spare glider assigned.

Marshalling and Despatch

Paratroop Operations

28. Marshalling procedure is to be the standard plan except where local conditions do not allow. Each airfield is to adopt the following standard despatching system. The Despatching Officer is to give the executive signals to the pilot to taxi and take off.

Glider Operations

29. Marshalling procedure is to be standard and is to be as follows, where conditions permit.

30. Gliders are to be marshalled on the runway in two parallel lines with tow-ropes and inter-comm already attached at both ends and tested. Tugs are to be marshalled on either side of the runway at an angle of 45° to take off direction, on hard surface aprons where provided, Tugs are to be positioned that the minimum of tow-rope slack remains to be taken up. The leading tug is to be on the runway with tow rope taut ready for take off.

31. Where local conditions do not permit the above method, or where the runway length is insufficient to accommodate the entire lift, some or all of the gliders and tugs are to be fed on to the runway by the quickest possible means. Where suitable feeder tracks exist, tugs are to be fed in along those tracks. The time lost by this slower method of marshalling can be reduced by having well drilled rope handling parties to attach tow ropes and by having marked places on the runway for the tug and glider positions.

Glider Despatch:

32. A Towmaster, provided by the Glider Pilot Regiment or R.A.F. Glider Squadron, is to stand by the glider where he is plainly visible to the pilot. He is to signal to the Control Officer by amber light, or flag when each glider is ready. The Control Officer is to give amber to taxi forward as soon as he judges it safe to do so. Immediately the rope slack is taken up, the Towmaster is to give GREEN or flag signal waved above the head to the Control Officer. If the runway is clear the Control Officer is to give GREEN to the tug pilot to take off. Red light or flag – stop. By night, an Assistant Control Officer is to stand along the runway at the estimated position where the tug becomes airborne, and is to fire a RED verey light if this runway becomes obstructed

33. In the event of engine failure in the tug or premature release for any reason, or of a swing during take off, the slider is to saying off the runway to the opposite side to that used by the tug, providing there is sufficient space to land within the airfield. The question as to the time at which the tug swings off or whether it continues to take off must be left to the discretion of the captain of aircraft. If the runway is not

cleared, the Assistant Control Officer and/or control officer is to give RED to any tug about to take off. The Glider Pilot and the Senior Passenger are to be clearly briefed against this contingency, as to whether:—

(a) The glider, if undamaged, should be returned to the take off point, or

(b) The passengers and/or load should be transferred to a reserve glider.

34. The Control Officers and Towmaster are to be fully qualified and experienced and are to have the necessary other rank assistance. The Assistant Control Officer is to have telephone communication with the Control Officer, and the Control Officer with the Command Post.

FORMING UP IN THE AIR

Paratroop Operations

[. . .]

(a) C.47 or C.53 Aircraft (USAAF or RAF)

(i) Twenty (20) minutes from the D.Z., the pilot is to tell the Stick Commander "PREPARE FOR ACTION STATIONS". The Stick Commander is to decide when to order the men "STAND UP"; on this order the men are to adjust parachutes and individual equipment. Nos. 2, 4 and 6 of the stick are to fold down the starboard rear seat. Troops are then to form single or slightly staggered file, facing aft, and then the Stick Commander is to order "HOOK UP". The Stick Commander is then to order "CHECK EQUIPMENT". Each man then checks himself and the man either side of him. The Stick Commander is to go down the fuselage and carry out a final check of each parachutist's equipment and hooking up; he then checks his own equipment and hooks himself up. [. . .] The Despatcher, on order from the Stick Commander, removes and stows away the door (if not already removed).

(ii) **Four (4) minutes from the D.Z.** the pilot is to turn on the red light which will remain on until the green light is turned on. This means "ACTION STATIONS" and the Stick Commander orders "STAND TO THE DOOR" whereupon troops are to form up for jumping. On the red light, the Despatcher is to take up position forward of the door, wearing his inter-comm. helmet, so as to provide an alternative means of communication in the event of the green light failing at the last moment.

(iii) **When over the D.Z.,** with the aircraft at the proper altitude, the green light is to turned on and remain on until it is no longer safe to jump when the red light is to be longer safe to jump when the red light is to be turned on again. Switching on the green light is a command to go, at that instant, in the order laid down. As the troops move down the fuselage, each man must guide his loose static line down the static attachment cable, with his left hand until he is third man from the floor; there he must throw it aside, and make his way to the door and step out.

(iv) Before take off and preferably at briefing, the Stick Commander is to instruct the Despatcher in the correct order for releasing the containers.

[. . .]

PATHFINDER PROCEDURE

46. All crews are to be trained for pathfinder operations and all aircraft are to be equipped with the necessary navigational aids.

47. A Marker force normally precedes the first aircraft of the main force by approx. 30 minutes, or as mutually agreed between the R.A.F. and Army Commander. This Force is to drop in the D.Z./L.Z. area and set up ground aids for the main force, i.e. radar aids, lights and/or ground strips.

48. The main force is to be prepared to drop as scheduled even though the above mentioned ground aids are not present. As the Marker force may have been prevented by cherry action from setting up ground aids, complete reliance is not to be placed upon them. If the ground situation makes it inadvisable to use pathfinders the leading echelon or the main force may be required to set up ground aids.

Marking of a D.Z. by Day

49. The standard day marking of each D.Z. is to consist of a panel T., a code letter and smoke signals. Both the T and the code letter (which letter is to identify the D.Z. and distinguish it from others in the same area), are to be constructed from panels or ground strips, each panel or strip measuring 3 ft. (three feet) by 15 feet (fifteen feet). Six panel strips are to be used, three (3) across the top of the T and three (3) forming the stem. Panels are to be spaced one panel length apart.

NOTE: It should be noted that the direction of the T does not necessarily indicate the direction of the wind. It is related to the direction of the run-in of aircraft from the Target R.V.

The colour and size of the T is to be dependent upon the size of the cleared area, vegetation and any trees obstructing vision, and is to be agreed upon by the Air and Army Commanders. Coloured smoke (other than yellow, orange, red or white) is to be employed, to indicate the position of the T. Colour coding of smoke signals is to be decided upon by the Air and Army Commanders. The T is to be positioned with due regard to wind speed and direction, shape and size of D.Z. and in order that it may be readily observed from aircraft running in from Target R.V. to D.Z. The identifying letter is to be placed in any suitable position in close proximity to the T.

50. When one stream or formation is being flown, the Eureka Radar beacon is to be placed within a radius of 100 yards from the T. advantage being taken of high ground and unobstructed line of sight to aircraft.

51. When two streams are being employed a Eureka Beacon, is to be placed in position for each stream, so that each stream will fly in parallel to the stem of the T., i.e. a total of 800 yards between beacons. Smoke signals are to be placed near the base of the stem of the T with due regard to the wind so that smoke will not obscure the T or the identifying letter. The axis of the T is to be parallel to the line of flight, with approach up the stem.

52. The Jump signal is to be given when the air-craft are over or level with the head of the T.

Marking of D.Z. by Night

53. The standard night marking for each D.Z. is to consist of lights forming a T made up of at least four (4) Holophane lights across the top and three (3) to the stem, each twenty-five (25) yards apart; lights to be red, green or amber, and with 1800 screening. The number and colour of the lights in the T at each D.Z. to be agreed upon between the Airborne and Air Commanders, to meet conditions encountered. The tail light of the T is to be the code light.

Marking of Landing Zones by Day

54. The day marking of Glider Landing Zones are to be by panel Ts, panel code letters, and coloured smoke. Panels are to measure fifteen (15) by three (3) feet. The T is to be placed as for D.Zs with the stem parallel to the line of glider landing, and so as to be readily observed from aircraft running in from Target R.V, to L.Z. The direction of landing so indicated is to be not more than 90° out of wind the amount depending on wind strength and configuration of L.Z – the best compromise being adopted.

55. Smoke is to be placed in the same manner as for a Dropping Zone; the colours yellow, orange, red or white will not be used.

56. The Eureka Beacon or Beacons are to be placed so as to bring aircraft to within visual distance of the T. The position or beacon should be related to the direction of run-in of aircraft from Target R.V. so that tugs will have only small as no alteration of course after sighting the T to fly to the point of release. Radar beacons are to be set up as soon as possible. They should be working 8 minutes before time of arrival of aircraft and none latitude up to ½ mile is permissible as regards position in order to achieve this. Advantage should be taken of high ground and unobstructed

line of sight to aircraft. Codeletters including L.Zs are to be prepared from panels similar to those used for marking the T.

Marking of a Landing Zone by Night

57. The following marking Glider Landing Zones by night presupposes sufficient light for glider pilots to distinguish individual fields for landings as briefed.

58. Night marking of Glider L.Zs is to be by a T formed of two (2) Holophane lights across the top, 50 yards apart and at least five lights forming the stem, twenty-five (25) yards apart. A red code light is to be placed 200 yards below the stem of the T and is to show through 360 degrees.

59. Lights to be red, green or amber and with 180° screening. The position of the T and of the Eureka(s) is to be the same as in the marking of L.Zs by day.

CHAPTER 5
ACHIEVING THE OBJECTIVE

Getting safely down on the ground, in roughly the right place, was an encouraging start to an airborne operation, but the real work lay ahead in achieving all mission objectives. Furthermore, although cumulatively paratroopers of different nationalities made numerous combat jumps between 1940 and 1945, we must acknowledge that most paratroopers spent their time and blood fighting as elite ground troops. Most of the German airborne divisions, for example, were ultimately either wiped out or crippled on the Eastern Front, in Italy and on the Western Front, with many of the soldiers going to their graves having never worn a parachute in action. So, as much as we remember the *Fallschirmjäger* for their airborne operations at places such as Eben Emael and Crete, we also remember them for their central part in, say, the four-month defence of Monte Cassino and the Gustav Line in January–May 1944, defending against a massive Allied superiority in firepower and troops.

The capabilities of the German paratroopers were a source of interest to the Allied intelligence services, especially as front-line reports indicated that the *Fallschirmjäger* had superior fighting skills, worth emulating. The following three American intelligence sources therefore reflect on how the German paras lived, fought and were organised. Of particular interest is the "Parachutist's Ten Commandments", which goes some way to explaining the distinct *esprit de corps* that sustained the *Fallschirmjäger* morale through both good times and bad.

From 'Parachutists (German)' (September 1942)

a. Introduction

A good many American fighting men have said that they would like to get a clearer mental picture of German parachutists—what they look like, how they train, what their standard tactics are, and in general how they do their job.

A common mistake is to imagine that the German parachutist is an ordinary infantryman who, on landing, goes into combat as a guerrilla fighter operating by himself, with help from any fellow-parachutists he may have the luck to meet. Actually, a German parachutist is a thoroughly trained specialist who fights as part of a well-organized unit. The German Army teaches him to believe that his is the most important of all jobs—that he is even more valuable than the aces of the German Air Force. After he has had a long, tough training in a parachutists' school, he is prepared not merely to jump well, but also to fight well. In fact, teamwork is the German parachutist's guiding principle.

b. Training

In choosing men who are to be sent to a parachutists' school, the German Army selects candidates who are young, athletic, quick-witted, and aggressive. Many of them are chosen with regard to certain special abilities (medical, engineering, and so on) which are just as much needed in parachute operations as in any other kind. During the training, emphasis is placed on exact procedures; for instance, a man packs a parachute with special care if he knows that he himself is going to use it. After proper physical conditioning, the candidate works from a jumping tower, practicing landing methods under different conditions. The school also requires, and develops, fearlessness; to illustrate, in a transport plane any sign of hesitation at the command "Jump!" may cost the candidate his membership in a parachute company.

However, parachute jumping is only a small part of the candidate's training, inasmuch as the German Army hopes to make him a useful member of a crack combat organization. He must know how to take part in what is called a "vertical envelopment"—that is, the capture of an area by air-borne troops.

c. Tactics

Airfields and railway and highway junctions are likely to be among the foremost objectives of vertical envelopments. Usually they begin at dawn. To make the parachutist's task less difficult, the Germans send out bombers, dive bombers, and fighters ahead of time to place fire on the defenders' gun positions and to drive gun crews to cover. Special attention is paid to antiaircraft batteries.

After an hour or more of continuous air attack, one of several possible events may take place, since German tactics at this stage are not standardized. If reconnaissance has shown that the terrain is favorable, gliders may descend and try to land their troops (usually ten to a glider) in a surprise move under cover of the air attack.

If the landings are successful, the glider-borne troops will make every effort to kill or capture the defending gun crews, thereby paving the way still further for the arrival of the parachute troops. Or, it may be that gliders will not be used at all, and that parachutists will be required to perform this operation by themselves. Much will depend on how strong the Germans think the ground defenses are.

Even though the parachutists will use tommy guns, rifles, or grenades while they are descending, experience has shown that this is the time when the defending ground forces will get the best possible results with their fire power. The Germans cannot aim effectively while they are descending. As they are nearing the ground, and for the first few minutes after they land, they make ideal targets. In Crete, for example, the Germans suffered enormous losses at this stage. Nevertheless, it must be remembered that if there is an airfield to be gained, the Germans apparently will sacrifice their parachutists freely in a concentrated effort to put the defenders' gun crews out of action. The German command will be chiefly interested in gaining enough control of an airfield to permit the landing of big transport aircraft like the Junkers 52s, which carry twelve men (plus the pilot, observer, and reserve pilot) or heavy equipment and fewer men. If the parachutists cannot overcome the defenders' gun crews, the operation is likely to be a failure from the German point of view. To put it briefly, the parachutists (perhaps supported by glider-borne troops) are shock troops, and it is upon their fighting that future control of the airfield hinges.

Different German tactics may be expected, however, when a parachute unit is dropped on an area which in itself may not interest the Germans, but which may be reasonably near an airfield, a junction, or a communications center. In this case, whatever units are dropped will quickly try to assemble as a coordinated fighting force and then advance to carry out their mission.

The German method of releasing parachutists from transport planes over any given area is so carefully worked out that very little is left to luck. The planes are likely to arrive in flights of three. Arriving over their objectives, they may circle, and then fly at an altitude of 300 to 500 feet across the area where the parachutists are to land. Jumping is carried out in formation. An officer in the leading plane shows a yellow flag two minutes before jumping as a sign to get ready. Half a minute before the jump, he shows a red and white flag. When the planes are over the area he pulls in the red and white flag. This is the signal to jump. If he waves both flags, crossing them back and forth, he is signalling "Don't jump!" At night, signals are given by colored flashlights, in which case red may mean "Get ready," green may mean "Half a minute to go," and white may mean "Jump!"

A leader in each plane gives the signal to jump by sounding an instrument like an automobile horn. Before jumping, the parachutists attach the ring of their parachutes to a wire running along the interior length of the aircraft on the right-hand side. The jump is made through the right-hand door, the ring yanking the cord of the parachute, which opens automatically after a 5-second delay (equal to a drop of about 80 feet). Equipment containers are dropped through the door on the left-hand side of the plane. Each container includes the equipment of three or four men, and is thrown out when, or just after, the men jump. The twelve men and four containers carried by each plane are supposed to be dropped within 9 to 10 seconds. When there is a delay, or when all the parachutists cannot jump while the plane is over the desired area, the plane will swing around in a circle and make a second run across the area.

Jumping at an altitude of 300 to 500 feet, the parachutists will reach the ground within 20 to 30 seconds.

The Germans have found it useful to attach parachutes of different colors to different kinds of loads. For example, a soldier's parachute may be a mixture of green and brown, to make him less conspicuous on the ground and to serve later as camouflage for captured motor vehicles. On the other hand, white parachutes may be used for equipment containers and pink for medical supplies. The Germans are likely to change the meaning of these colors from time to time. Since parachutists can request extra supplies by laying strips of white cloth on the ground in certain formations, there is always a possibility that the opposition will find out the code, and deceive German aircraft into dropping such supplies as ammunition, food, and medicine.

d. Organization of Division

A brief discussion of how the German Flight Division VII—nicknamed the "Parachute Division"—was organized at the time of the capture of Crete will show some of the elements that may be expected in a German parachute attack. In May 1941, Flight Division VII was composed of the following units:

Division Headquarters.

Three parachute regiments.

Parachute machine-gun battalion (three companies).

Parachute antitank battalion (three companies).

Parachute antiaircraft and machine-gun battalion (three companies).

Parachute artillery battery (three troops, four guns each).

Parachute engineer battalion.

Parachute signal unit.

Parachute medical unit.

Parachute supply unit.

Captured loading lists indicated a standard organization of 144 parachutists per company, carried in twelve aircraft, arranged in four flights of three aircraft each.

Before an attack, a parachute regiment may be reorganized to make its fire power more even. An exchange of platoons may be made between rifle companies and machine-gun and bomb-thrower companies so that, after the reorganization, each company may have, for example, two rifle platoons, a heavy machine-gun platoon, and a platoon of heavy bomb throwers.

e. The Parachutist's "Ten Commandments"

Here is a translation of a document captured from a German parachute trooper who was taken prisoner in Greece. Its title is "The Parachutist's Ten Commandments."

1. You are the elite of the German Army. For you, combat shall be fulfillment. You shall seek it out and train yourself to stand any test.

2. Cultivate true comradeship, for together with your comrades you will triumph or die.

3. Be shy of speech and incorruptible. Men act, women chatter; chatter will bring you to the grave.

4. Calm and caution, vigor and determination, valor and a fanatical offensive spirit will make you superior in attack.

5. In facing the foe, ammunition is the most precious thing. He who shoots uselessly, merely to reassure himself, is a man without guts. He is a weakling and does not deserve the title of parachutist.

6. Never surrender. Your honor lies in Victory or Death.

7. Only with good weapons can you have success. So look after them on the principle—First my weapons, then myself.

8. You must grasp the full meaning of an operation so that, should your leader fall by the way, you can carry it out with coolness and caution.

9. Fight chivalrously against an honest foe; armed irregulars deserve no quarter.

10. With your eyes open, keyed up to top pitch, agile as a greyhound, tough as leather, hard as Krupp steel, you will be the embodiment of a German warrior.

From 'Ground Tactics of German Paratroops' (June 1944)

The commander of a German parachute demonstration battalion recently issued to his companies a directive which affords useful insight into some of the ground tactics that enemy paratroopers may be expected to employ. The following extracts from the battalion commander's order are considered especially significant:

1. For parachute and air-landing operations, I have given orders for section leaders and their seconds-in-command to carry rifles, and for the No. 3 men on the light machine guns to carry machine carbines. There are tactical reasons for this decision. The section commander must be able to point out targets to his section by means of single tracer rounds. The No. 3 man on the light machine gun must be able to give this gun covering fire from his machine carbine in the event that close combat takes place immediately after landing. This last should be regarded as a distinct possibility. He must provide this covering fire until the light machine gun is in position and ready to fire. Before the assault, the No. 3 man on the light machine gun must also be able to beat off local counterattacks with his machine carbine until the machine gun is ready to go into action.

2. Since so many targets are likely to be seen only for a fleeting moment, and since the rifleman himself must disappear from hostile observation as soon as he has revealed his position by firing, the German paratrooper must be extremely skillful at "snap shooting" (rapid aiming and firing). The following three points are to be noted and put into practice:

a. Snap shooting is most useful at short ranges. It will not be employed at ranges of more than 330 yards, except in close combat and defense, when it will generally be employed at ranges under 1,100 yards.

b. Even more important than rapid aiming and firing is rapid disappearance after firing, no matter what the range may be.

c. Movement is revealing, also. Men must move as little as possible and must quickly find cover from fire at each bound.

3. I leave to company commanders the distribution of automatic and sniper rifles within companies. I wish only to stress the following principles:

a. Wherever possible, sniper and automatic rifles will be given to those paratroopers who can use them most effectively. In general practice, this rules out commanders and headquarters personnel (who have duties other than firing).

b. There seems to be a general but incorrect impression that our sniper rifles improve the marksmanship of men who are only moderately good shots. These rifles are provided with telescopes only to make more distinct those targets which are not clearly visible to the naked eye. This means that an advantage accrues solely to very good marksmen firing at medium ranges—and, what is more, only where impact can be observed and the necessary adjustments made. Since the sniper is seldom in a position where he can observe for himself, a second man, with binoculars, generally will be detailed to work with the sniper.

4. I wish company commanders to make the report on the battle of Crete the subject of continual reference in their own lectures, and in the lectures of platoon commanders who are training noncoms. I particularly desire that those passages in the report which deal with the importance of the undertaking as a whole be drilled into every man. The last three exercises I have attended have shown me that this principle is by no means evident to all platoon commanders. Platoon commanders in this battalion are still too much inclined to fight their own private brands of war instead of paying attention to the larger picture.

5. It is extremely likely that, during a parachute or air-landing operation, this battalion will land in hostile positions not previously reconnoitered, and will have to fight for the landing area. Such fighting will be carried out according to the same regulations which would obtain if we had fought our way into the heart of a hostile position.

6. Inasmuch as we shall soon be receiving our new machine guns, training with those new machine guns we already have must be pushed forward in our light companies—at least to the extent of giving the No. 1 men about 1 1/2 hours a day on it. The most important point to be driven home is that this weapon is to be fired in very short bursts to avoid waste of ammunition.

7. During the exercises and field firing demonstrations I have witnessed—I admit they have been few—I did not once see yellow identification panels used to mark our forward line, nor did I see the swastika flags used to identify our own troops to friendly aircraft. Henceforth, these panels and flags will be carried on all occasions and will be spread out at the proper times.

8. I wish platoon exercises to include more emphasis on the attacks on well prepared defensive positions. This Will Include cooperation between two assault detachments and a reserve assault ("mopping-up") detachment.

Each German paratroop company commander, it is reported, must designate five to seven of his best men as a tank-hunting detachment. These men perform their regular duties, but are prepared to act as a team in their tank-hunting capacity whenever they may be called upon. The infantry training of German paratroopers is usually very thorough, covering all normal training and, in some instances, use of the light machine gun, heavy machine gun, mortar, and antitank rifle, as well. Cunning and initiative are stressed. Many men are taught to drive tanks and other vehicles. Use of simple demolitions and the handling of antitank and antipersonnel mines are often included in the training.

From 'How Paratroops Clear Fields for Gliders' (June 1944)

German paratroopers conduct a rapid assault from a DFS 230 glider.

1. INTRODUCTION

The Germans are well aware that troops dropped by parachute must be supplied rapidly with sufficient reinforcements, equipment, ammunition, and rations if the average paratroop operation is to have a fighting chance of success. To achieve this, the Germans stipulate that the first mission of certain designated paratroopers, on landing in the jump area, is to improvise a landing field for gliders. Reinforcement by air-landing troops is the first use to which an improvised field is put. Supplies which cannot be dropped are landed next. After this, the Germans try to establish an organized supply system, which will include full protection of the supplies arriving and an orderly distribution to the troops.

2. RECONNAISSANCE FOR SUITABLE FIELDS

If German paratroops are forced to engage in combat immediately upon hitting the ground or shortly afterward, the designated soldiers attempt to reconnoiter for suitable landing fields not too far from the area in which fighting is in progress, and yet, wherever possible, out of range of hostile fire. The German preference is for a field near a road or path leading to the fighting troops. It is regarded as essential that the surrounding obstacles permit a glide of at least "1 in 15." An effort is made to provide each regiment with one glider landing field having at least two landing strips. The object is to allow a number of gliders to land simultaneously. An ideal field, the Germans specify, is one which permits gliders to land regardless of the direction in which the wind is blowing.

The Germans regard the following as unfavorable features: very rocky, uneven ground; stony ground where the stones go deeper than 2 feet and consequently are hard to remove; swampy or wooded ground; ground with thick vegetation, ditches, stone walls, hedges, wire fences, and so on.

The following, on the other hand, are described as favorable features: moderately soft ground with grass; ground with tall grass and even a little vegetation; farm land, even if furrowed; corn fields (which are fairly easy to clear); and sandy ground, even if it is somewhat pebbly.

Besides the above, the prevailing wind direction also influences the German choice of a field.

3. CONSTRUCTION OF LANDING FIELDS

All obstacles are removed, not only from the landing strip, but from a zone 65 feet wide on each side of the strip. Uneven ground is leveled. Although normally every precaution is taken to lessen the danger of crash landings, the Germans follow an interesting procedure if time is very short or if the terrain presents great difficulties. Under these circumstances, the Germans clear at least one-third of the landing strip, on the principle that this much of a strip will at least decrease the speed of a glider somewhat after it touches the ground, and that crash landings will consequently be eased to some extent.

Just off the landing strips, parking areas are prepared for the gliders already landed. These parking areas are so arranged as not to hinder further development of the landing strip, in case this is ordered later. Vegetation stripped from the landing field is saved, and is used in camouflaging the parked gliders.

The center of the landing strip is marked with identification panels for air recognition, and the wind direction is shown by a large T made with panels and, indicated when necessary, by smoke as well.

Over the duration of the war, airborne tactics became increasing ambitious in terms of scale and objectives. From 1939 until early 1941, airborne assaults tended to have limited and localised objectives; airfields, bridges and fortresses were the principal targets. The German invasion of Crete broke that mould, making airborne warfare part of major operational thinking. Yet if anything, the larger operations (Crete, D-Day, Arnhem especially) also revealed the limits of airborne warfare – ambition always had to be tempered with realism. What was certain, however, was by 1942 airborne forces had a sharpening body of doctrine to guide planning. This is evident in the following text from American Field Manual 31-30. It explains in detail critical aspects such as offensive and defensive actions following landing, unit organisation and weapon deployment, plus addresses issues that could be surprisingly complex for paratroopers – such as how to manage enemy prisoners while on a dynamic operation with few men to spare.

From FM 31-30, *Tactics and Technique of Airborne Troops* **(1942)**

CHAPTER 3
TACTICAL OPERATIONS

27. General.—*a.* If the landing field at the final destination has been secured from hostile small-arms and artillery fire, the subsequent operations of air landing troops will not differ from those of similar units transported by any other method, except for lack of organic transportation and difficulty of supply. This chapter deals with landings of air-borne troops against active hostile opposition.

b. Operations of air landing troops which land shortly after the initial attack of parachute troops are characterized by—

(1) Speed.

(2) Initiative on the part of all commanders.

(3) Boldness, in order to take maximum advantage of initial surprise.

(4) Lack of supporting fires except by combat aviation.

28. Activities Immediately Upon Landing.—*a.* Although loading plans will maintain the integrity of tactical units to the greatest extent possible, it will be necessary for leaders of all units above the squad to regain control of their units before proceeding on their missions. This may be accomplished by means of a rendezvous or rallying point selected in advance from maps or aerial photographs. This position should afford cover from small-arms fire. Units having specific missions leave their rendezvous area as soon as the last element reports.

Supplies are dropped to US troops of the 101st Airborne Division, besieged in Bastogne in the winter of 1944.

b. Immediately upon landing, troops deplane under orders of the senior officer or noncommissioned officer in the plane. Wherever possible, all supplies and equipment are unloaded by the personnel as they leave the plane. As soon as unloaded, all personnel immediately leave for the initial rallying point or rendezvous of their imit. After the first few flights have landed, men are detailed to meet planes carrying supplies or equipment in order that they may be unloaded promptly and enabled to take off.

c. Upon deplaning, troops immediately assume a deployed formation. Weapons must be instantly available for use. In moving from the landing area to rendezvous or assembly area approach march formations are used. In assembly positions and whenever troops halt, they must be immediately disposed for all around defense. Where natural cover is not available they must promptly dig in. Men armed with antitank grenades are included in each echelon. They must be particularly alert for individual tanks or other armored vehicles which may have been dug in and concealed near the field. Antitank gims should be brought in as early as practicable.

d. As each unit is assembled its commander sends a report to the next higher unit. This report will advise the higher commander of any casualties the unit has suffered and the fact that it has proceeded on its scheduled mission, or will state briefly any changes made as a result of the situation existing upon arrival.

e. Men from the first elements of a unit will be posted as guides to insure that elements arriving by later flights are directed to the proper rendezvous.

f. A staff officer, arriving on one of the early planes, should meet commanders of later units to acquaint them with the current situation and advise them of any change of plan required. In addition, this officer should keep his own commander informed as to the condition and status of troops as they arrive.

g. An officer with sufficient assistants should be detailed by the task force commander to control all activities on the landing field. He and some of his assistants should arrive with the first echelon of the air landing troops. His principal mission is to insure rapid unloading of all planes and prompt clearing of the field of men, supplies, and planes in order to keep the landing area clear for succeeding echelons.

h. The commander of the parachute troops who have landed in the area details a liaison officer to contact the air landing troops. This officer will inform commanders of air landing troops of the status of parachute operations.

29. Attack to Gain Initial Objectives.—The attack of air landing troops to gain initial objectives will be conducted in accordance with detailed plans and orders issued prior to leaving the departure airport. Commanders of higher units will have little or no opportunity to influence these initial attacks. Regimental commanders and

staff officers can best influence the operation during this period by insuring orderly deplanement and assembly of reserve and supporting elements of the regiment.

30. Attack Beyond Initial Objectives.—*a.* General.—Attacks beyond the initial objectives should be coordinated. Generally they are initiated only on orders of the task force commander or his representative. However, interruption in communications between the task force commander and the commander on the ground may force the latter to decide upon his own initiative whether or not to continue the attack, beyond initial objectives. Before ordering a continuation of the attack on D-day, a commander must consider—

(1) The importance of exploiting to the maximum the initial advantage of surprise.

(2) The importance of the objective selected relative to the success of the operation.

(3) The necessity for occupation of strong defensive positions for the night.

(4) The plan of the task force commander, particularly as to time of landing of additional troops and for continuation of the attack after initial objectives are captured.

b. Objectives.—Objectives for attacks beyond initial objectives may be indicated in the mission assigned in the original order. When the commander on the ground must determine which of these subsequent objectives will best further accomplishment of the assigned mission or plans of the task force, he must consider the following:

(1) *Attack to contact troops landing in adjacent areas.*—In order to split enemy forces and conceal the principal effort of the attacker, as well as to permit an increased rate of arrival of troops in the area, two or more landing areas, separated by several miles, may be employed. In this situation the position of air landing forces will be much more secure once these separated forces have made personal contact. If an enemy force is interposed between these units, a prompt attack should be launched against this force by both landing units, unless previous instructions from the task force commander prohibit this action. It will rarely be possible for the separate commanders to coordinate their efforts initially, but they do so as soon as communication can be established.

(2) *Separation of elements of the enemy forces.*—Severance of communications between elements of the hostile forces will frequently have decisive effects. Strong consideration should be given to attack of objectives which will place the air landing troops between defending forces, and thus prevent movement of supplies and reinforcements from one force to the other.

(3) *Hostile artillery.*—Initial objectives of air landing troops should deny defending forces observation for artillery fire on the landing fields. However,

even unobserved artillery fire falling on a landing field may cause considerable destruction of materiel and planes. Therefore, every effort must be made to destroy all hostile artillery or to drive it beyond range of the landing field. Neutralization of this artillery is a suitable mission for supporting combat aviation.

c. Orders.—Orders for attacks by air landing troops beyond initial objectives are similar to orders for renewal of an attack by any ground forces. They must be clear and concise. They should be issued orally or as written messages in fragmentary form. Rarely will the situation permit subordinate commanders to be assembled to receive orders.

31. Night Dispositions.—*a.* Employment of air landing troops presupposes air superiority in the area. Movement of any considerable number of troops by the enemy should be extremely difficult if not impossible during daylight. This condition, together with the enemy's familiarity with the terrain, makes night attacks on his part most probable.

b. Plans and necessary reconnaissances for night defensive positions should be completed prior to darkness. These plans, whenever possible, should provide for night dispositions differing from those existing just prior to darkness. Strong outposts must be pushed forward, and patrolling to the front, flanks, and rear must be continuous and aggressive throughout the night.

32. Employment of Reserves.—Employment of reserves by air landing troops corresponds in general to that of any unit of similar size. Frequently, troops whose principal assignment in the operation is that of a reserve element may be employed initially on such missions as protecting the rear or flank of troops actively engaged.

33. Defense.—The mission assigned air landing troops is usually offensive in the initial phases of the operation. However, in many operations, such as seizing of a beach, bridgehead, or important communication center, once the initial objective has been captured the mission becomes one of holding the position pending arrival of other military or naval forces. Continuous fronts cannot be held. Dispositions must provide for defense of tactical localities by small units disposed for all around defense with the intervals covered by fire. In general, dispositions will approximate those of an outpost of a defensive position. All routes of communication must be covered. The small number of troops and lack of heavy supporting weapons must be compensated for by strong air support and effective air-ground communication.

34. Communications.—Owing to the normally wide dispersion of air landing forces and the rapidity of action essential for successful operation of these forces, communications are difficult to establish and maintain. Maximum use is made of all standard means of communication, together with such means as may be improvised. The various means of communication are employed as follows:

a. Messengers.—Extensive use is made of foot messengers, and of bicycle and motorcycle messengers using machines transported by air or captured. Special precautions are taken to insure that messengers understand where they are to go and what routes are safe for them to follow.

b. Telephones.—There will usually be little use for wire communication, owing to the weight of material, time necessary to install, abnormally wide fronts, and the rapidity of action of air landing infantry. Sound-powered equipment TE 11 is valuable for use by observation posts and for fire control of infantry mortars. In certain situations temporary use of local communications systems which have been seized may be practicable.

c. Radio.—Small portable voice radios of limited range are particularly valuable for air landing operations. Their use by units down to include platoons will greatly simplify the control problem for commanders. If the air landing force is smaller than a division, provision must be made to secure additional radio equipment with sufficient range to contact the task force commander and headquarters of the armored or other force which is to relieve it. Radio is also a principal means of contact with supporting combat aviation for battalions and larger units.

d. Panels.—In addition to normal panel procedure for communication with the air, companies and platoons of air landing troops that have special or independent missions employ simple panel codes prescribed by the task force commander to provide for target designation, to report their own locations, and to request needed supplies.

e. Pyrotechnics.—Use of pyrotechnics provides a valuable means of communi-cation with the air. Ground signal projectors. Very pistols, and ground flares may be used.

f. Pigeons.—Pigeons are used by air landing troops as an emergency means of communication.

35. Supply.—*a. General.*—Air landing operations are usually planned for a period of short duration. In general, sufficient supplies are carried initially to cover as much of the operation as possible. However, plans must provide for resupply by air for a considerable period. Owing to lack of transportation for hauling supplies after their delivery at landing fields, consideration must be given to dropping emergency supplies by parachutes.

b. Rations.—Pending development of a special ration for parachute troops and similar units, field ration D and field ration C will normally be issued for air landing operations. The D ration is carried on the person as an individual reserve. Not more than one C ration may also be carried initially by each man.

c. Water.—Except for operations in desert or semiarid regions, the problem of water supply is largely one of purification. Where water must be supplied by air, the five-gallon container is most satisfactory as it facilitates distribution.

d. Ammunition.—It is difficult to compute ammunition requirements of an air landing operation. All other supplies are held to a minimum in order that maximum amounts of ammunition may be carried with the troops. Arrangements must be made to have ample reserves immediately available at departure airfields for resupply by air. Parachutes and proper containers must be available for dropping emergency replenishment close to the troops. Supporting aviation should be particularly alert for calls for ammunition.

e. Medical supplies.—Owing to the difficulties of evacuation, medical supplies must be ample. Provision must be made for resupply by air.

f. Other supplies and equipment.—Since loss of some planes must be expected, it is essential that a reserve of additional essential articles of equipment be provided at a departure airport, in order that supplies or equipment such as radio sets, machine guns, automatic rifles, and antitank weapons which may be lost or destroyed can be replaced promptly.

36. Evacuation.—While evacuation of severely wounded by air is possible, loading of these cases would retain planes on the field for some time. Operations of air landing troops usually contemplate that contact will be effected with friendly ground forces within a few days. For these reasons plans usually will not provide for evacuation from the area of the air landing operation. Company aid men of battalion medical sections will accompany their companies. They should be provided with additional first-aid supplies.

Wounded men should be evacuated to battalion aid stations and thence to collecting stations near the landing areas. If the air landing force is smaller than a division, regimental medical detachments should be reinforced by additional men and material in order to care for casualties at these collecting stations.

37. Prisoners and Captured Civilians.—Arrangements must be made for control and guarding of prisoners and of civilians who are taken into custody. These may be employed in the unloading of supplies and material at the landing fields.

38. Conduct of Personnel.—All officers and noncommissioned officers must take prompt and effective action to insure exemplary conduct on the part of all members of the air landing force. Individuals who mistreat civilians or violate property rights, or whose conduct is in violation of instructions, will be dealt with promptly.

[. . .]

42. OPERATIONS—*a. General.*—Parachute troops may be considered the spearhead of a vertical envelopment or the advance guard element of air landing troops or other forces. They must seek decisive action immediately upon landing. Success depends largely upon rapid execution of missions assigned to subordinate units. Prompt, decisive, and intelligent leadership is of great importance. Failure of one of the smaller units to accomplish its mission may mean defeat of the entire parachute command involved.

b. Surprise.—There is no field of military endeavor in which surprise is of greater importance than in parachute operations. Surprise in some form is a prerequisite to success. It may be obtained in various ways. For example, the enemy may be surprised by the locality selected for the attack, the density of parachutists per given area, or by the type of weapons with which the parachutists are equipped.

c. Objectives and time limitations.—Parachute troops are assigned specific missions and limited objectives. Initially they can be directly supported only by aviation. Since they are limited to their individual equipment and such equipment and supplies as can be dropped from the air, they cannot hold objectives for long periods. The maximum time they can hold an objective depends largely upon the hostile situation and reaction, and upon the effectiveness of their air support. Consequently, parachute troops are used to seize objectives pending the prompt arrival of other forces, or to seize objectives which are to be destroyed and abandoned.

d. Type of combat.—Parachute troops are usually required to seize a designated locality by rapid offensive action. This is generally followed by defensive action to hold the locality pending arrival of air landing troops or ground forces.

e. Control.—Because of the unavoidable dispersion incident to mass parachute jumping, and the necessity for speed, initial combat takes the form of quick, aggressive, coordinated action by individuals and small groups. Direction, coordination, and control can be effected only by careful planning. Orders of all parachute units must stress flexibility of operation.

43. Principles of Employment.—The following considerations govern employment of parachute troops:

a. The element of surprise must be present.

b. Parachute troops should not be used for missions that can be performed by other roops.

c. Decision to use parachute troops should be made well in advance of the scheduled date of the operation.

d. A comprehensive knowledge of the terrain involved in the operation is essential.

e. A long range forecast of meteorological conditions should be carefully considered during the planning phase.

f. Because of technical requirements, all parachute troop missions should start from a base which affords the required facilities for packing of parachutes and for making minor repairs. From this base, parachute units may be flown directly to their objective or transported by any available means to a designated air field, to be picked up by their transport airplanes.

g. Terrain objectives to be seized and held should lie in the path of the contemplated advance of friendly forces.

h. Local air superiority must exist.

i. Combat aviation is essential for the protection of parachute troops while in flight and during landing, and for supporting fires before, during, and after landing.

j. Parachute troops should be relieved and withdrawn to their base as soon as practicable after arrival of supporting ground forces.

k. All principles of offensive and defensive action applying to infantry combat are equally applicable to parachute troops.

44. Terrain.—a. Conformation.—The character of the terrain is of prime importance in parachute operations. Clear cultivated fields, free of power lines and similar obstructions, are ideal landing areas. However, parachute units can jump in areas containing scattered woods, with little, if any, resultant loss in combat effectiveness. Large trees, stumps, rocks, or similar obstructions are unquestionably jumping hazards, but they are not insurmountable obstacles. Since cleared areas are likely to be defended more strongly than areas containing hazards to parachute jumping, the number of casualties caused by ground defenders will be greater when the jumps are made in cleared areas. All parachute units should be prepared to jump in difficult terrain.

b. Size of landing areas.—(1) The size of landing areas required depends largely upon the size of the unit jumping, formation of the planes, and efficiency of pilots and jump- masters. A platoon will usually require a landing area approximately 250 yards wide by 600 yards long. If all men are to be jumped in one passage over the area, 8 to 12 seconds are required for men and equipment to clear the plane. If additional flights successively follow the first platoon at approximately 1,000 yards (or 20 seconds) until an entire battalion has jumped, the time between the first jump and the landing of the last man should not exceed 5 minutes. With this formation a battalion jumps one platoon at a time over the same landing area, and the battalion pattern on the ground should not exceed 800 by 1,200 yards. Experience has shown that the battalion landing area will have a larger pattern than a platoon area because of the large cumulative pilot error occurring when many transports fly in a column formation.

(2) Variations in the flight formation have a direct bearing on the pattern and on the jump time. For example, a formation may be employed in which each flight of three planes (one platoon of parachute troops) is in V formation, the flights for each company are in staggered line, and each company follows successively in column. The battalion usually jumps a company at a time from this formation. Because of better control and closer formation of the planes, the battalion pattern on the ground should not exceed 500 by 800 yards, and the jump time should not exceed two minutes.

ORGANIZATION AND TECHNIQUE OF PARACHUTE UNITS

Section I

GENERAL

48. General.—The vital need for flexibility in parachute units demands that the smaller components be as nearly self-sustaining as possible. This, in turn, requires that each individual in the squad be capable of performing the duties of any other member of the squad. In addition, every member of a parachute platoon should be able to fire effectively all types of weapons in the platoon. Since administrative personnel of parachute troops do not accompany the combat units, all personnel having duties incident to mess, administration, and supply are concentrated in battalion or regimental headquarters. In general, the duties of commanders, leaders of small units, and staff officers correspond to those of analogous personnel in the rifle regiment. In addition, they have certain other duties peculiar to parachute troops, as indicated hereafter.

Section II

PARACHUTE RIFLE SQUAD

49. Composition.—The parachute rifle squad consists of two noncommissioned officers (a sergeant and a corporal) and ten privates. The sergeant commands the squad and may act as jumpmaster; the corporal assists the squad leader.

50. Armament and Equipment.—Armament of a rifle squad includes ten rifles, a submachine gun, and a light machine gun. These weapons, together with equipment as prescribed by Table of Basic Allowances No. 7, are dropped in delivery units.

51. Duties of the Squad Leader.—The squad leader is responsible for the conduct and equipment of his squad and for execution of the platoon leader's orders. He supervises and inspects the packing of all parachutes. He checks and inspects the packing of his squad equipment in supply containers and inspects the squad immediately prior to enplaning. When so instructed by his platoon commander he divides his squad into half squads or other subdivisions in such manner as to take advantage of the special qualifications, training, and other characteristics of the

individuals. When separated from his platoon leader during combat, he acts on his own initiative and assumes full responsibility for the squad.

52. Missions.—*a.* When operating as part of a larger unit, the missions of the parachute squad are substantially the same as those for any other infantry squad. However, the parachute squad usually is given much greater freedom of action than the infantry squad and may act independently.

b. Exceptionally, the parachute squad, the half squad, or even individuals may be assigned independent missions which involve operations deep in the enemy's rear areas. Usually no support is planned for such operations; however, possible routes and methods of escape are carefully planned in advance. The tasks assigned ordinarily involve demolitions, such as destruction of a factory, a key railroad bridge, a vital dock facility, a critical communication center, or other important enemy installations. Such mission can be accomplished only by secrecy, surprise, and utmost speed of execution.

53. Assembly Points.—Immediately upon landing, the individual soldier is trained to proceed to the designated assembly point of his squad or subdivision. This procedure should be habitual. Exceptions will occur only when individuals are assigned initial missions away from the squad.

54. Supply of Equipment and Ammunition.—*a. Initial.*—Except for hand grenades and a small amount of ammunition for pistols or other light weapons, carried by descending parachutists, the initial ammunition supply for the squad is dropped in the delivery units that carry its other weapons. At least one day's supply for each weapon is dropped simultaneously with the squad. Delivery units for each group must be landed close to it. Delivery units are clearly marked to indicate their contents and the group to which they belong. Delivery unit parachutes may be marked by the use of colored canopies. However, the colors of canopies should be varied in different operations so that a canopy a certain color will not always indicate the same piece of equipment. For deception, colored canopies may be used occasionally for personnel. Equipment containers are marked by colored coverings, smoke signals, colored streamers, or other readily recognized devices.

b. Packing and loading.—The squad packs prescribed arms, equipment, and supplies in delivery units under supervision of the platoon leader. Prior to enplaning, these delivery units are placed in equipment racks or loaded in the plane under supervision of the jumpmaster.

c. Subsequent supply.—When the squad is acting alone, the squad leader makes requests upon supporting aviation for his needs by means of prearranged signals.

55. Ration and Water Supply.—Appropriate field rations and water for at least one day are dropped in delivery units containing the weapons for each subgroup of

the squad. Class D rations may be carried by the individual jumper. When two or more days' rations are desired, and space in the unit delivery units is not sufficient, these extra rations may be dropped in a separate delivery unit along with those containing weapons, and picked up by troops when the situation permits.

[. . .]

Section III

PARACHUTE 60-MM MORTAR SQUAD

Fig. 13. 60-mm mortar, submachine gun, and rifles displayed on an A-5 type aerial delivery unit.

60. Composition.—The mortar squad consists of one sergeant, squad leader, and five privates, first class—a gunner, assistant gunner, and three ammunition bearers.

61. Armament and Equipment.—The armament of a parachute 60-mm mortar squad consists of one 60-mm mortar, one submachine gun, and three rifles.

Section IV

PARACHUTE RIFLE PLATOON

63. Composition.—The parachute rifle platoon consists of a command group, two rifle squads, and one mortar squad. The command group consists of platoon leader, second-in-command, platoon sergeant, signal corporal, radio operator, and two messengers.

64. Duties of Personnel.—*a.* The commander of a parachute platoon performs the duties of an infantry rifle platoon commander, and in addition is responsible—

(1) That the condition of all parachute equipment of his platoon is satisfactory.

(2) For thorough inspection of all parachute jumping and training equipment used by his platoon, with particular attention to all details concerning the safety of individuals.

(3) For supervision of the inspection of parachute equipment prescribed in paragraph 86.

(4) For constant observation of all members of his platoon in order to detect any prejudicial physical or mental deficiencies.

(5) For designation of the order in which his squads jump, assembly point(s) after landing, and when appropriate, the rallying point for subsequent assembly.

(6) For efficient air-ground communication, if the platoon is acting alone.

(7) That all of his men are thoroughly acquainted with the platoon mission and with their individual or group missions.

(8) For designation of men to operate any special weapons or equipment involved in the mission, and for supervising their training.

b. The second-in-command assists the platoon leader and performs such duties as he directs.

c. The signal corporal is in charge of all means of signal communications within the platoon.

d. In general, the platoon sergeant and messengers perform the duties described for corresponding personnel in the rifle platoon of a rifle regiment. The radio operator accompanies the platoon leader.

Section V

PARACHUTE 81-MM MORTAR PLATOON

65. Composition.—The parachute 81-mm mortar platoon consists of platoon headquarters and two sections.

66. Duties.—The commander of a parachute 81-mm mortar platoon performs the duties of an 81-mm mortar platoon commander in a rifle regiment, and in addition is responsible for items listed for the parachute rifle platoon commander.

Section VI

PARACHUTE CALIBER .30 MACHINE-GUN PLATOON

67. Composition.—The parachute caliber .30 machine-gun platoon consists of a headquarters and two sections.

68. Duties.—The commander of a parachute caliber .30 machine-gun platoon performs the duties of a caliber .30 machine-gun platoon commander in a rifle regiment, and in addition is responsible for items listed for the parachute rifle platoon commander.

Section VII

PARACHUTE RIFLE COMPANY

69. Composition.—The parachute rifle company consists of a command group and three rifle platoons. The command group consists of a company commander, a second-in-command, and a small group of enlisted men to assist the company commander in tactical control of the company, to operate communication equipment, and to protect the command post. There are no mess, supply, or office administrative personnel in the company. It has no rear echelon. All members of the company are qualified parachutists and accompany the unit into combat.

70. Armament and Equipment.—During descent all members of the command group carry the same equipment as members of the rifle squad.

71. Missions and Orders.—*a*. Owing to lack of centralized control during the initial phase of a parachute operation, and need for prompt action on the part of all units, the mission assigned to a parachute company usually requires independent action in the first phase of combat. When the company has taken its initial objective, or has reached the assembly area prescribed in the battalion order, its action is coordinated with that of the remainder of the battalion, either by provisions of the initial battalion order or by subsequent orders of the battalion commander.

b. The company commander assigns appropriate tasks to his subordinate units, being careful to leave to his subordinate leaders the utmost freedom of action consistent with the mission and the situation. In assigning these missions, he must take into consideration the difficult communication problems that confront the smaller parachute units in the initial stages of combat, and employ mission type orders.

c. In some situations the company commander can plan his operation and issue his initial orders in great detail. It is essential that provision be made for all contingencies that can reasonably be foreseen. As indicated in subparagraph *b* above, his orders to subordinate units must not, however. Impose unnecessary restrictions upon the Junior leaders nor attempt to control their actions too far into the future.

72. Duties of the Company Command Group.—Duties prescribed in FM 7-10 for individuals of a rifle company command group apply generally to corresponding members of a parachute company command group. All members of the command group accompany the commander and perform such duties as he directs.

73. Duties of the Parachute Company Commander.—The parachute company commander performs the duties prescribed for a rifle company commander in a rifle regiment, and in addition is charged with—

a. Supervising the inspections prescribed in paragraphs 56 and 86a and c.

b. Arranging for normal combat supply of his company in accordance with principles and methods stated in this manual.

c. Determining well in advance the need for special equipment and supplies, and making necessary arrangements to get them.

Section VIII

PARACHUTE BATTALION

74. Composition.—The parachute battalion consists of a battalion headquarters and headquarters company and three rifle companies. An 81-mm mortar platoon and a caliber .30 machine-gun platoon are organic parts of the headquarters company. The command group, from the battalion headquarters and headquarters company, is divided into a combat echelon and an administration echelon. The administration echelon includes mess and other rear echelon personnel.

75. Armament and Equipment.—Equipment carried during descent by members of the battalion combat echelon is the same as that carried by individuals of the rifle squad.

76. Supply and Jumping Technique.—The technique of packing, loading, and dropping equipment and supplies, and of jumping personnel in the various subordinate elements within the battalion, is similar to that prescribed for the rifle squad.

Section IX

PARACHUTE REGIMENT

77. Composition.—*a.* The parachute regiment consists of a headquarters and headquarters company, a service company, and three parachute battalions.

b. The composition and functions of the headquarters company correspond in general to the headquarters company of a rifle regiment, except that it contains special facilities to effect demolitions and has no reconnaissance platoon.

c. All motor transportation in the parachute regiment is assigned to the service company. This company also provides personnel and facilities for supply, parachute maintenance, and motor maintenance.

d. The combat echelon of the regimental command group consists of regimental commander, regimental executive, S-2, S-3, communication officer, and necessary enlisted assistants. The administration and supply echelon functions at the base from which the regiment is operating.

e. The commander of the parachute regiment is charged with the duties of a commander of an infantry rifle regiment. See FM 7-40. In addition, he is responsible for parachute activities and maintenance, and training peculiar to parachute troops.

f. If the tactical situation requires, larger parachute forces may be formed by the groupment of several parachute regiments.

SOURCES

CHAPTER 1

Air Ministry, CD.226, *The Parachute Training Manual* (March 1944) *Accessed at the National Archives AIR 10/3845*

CHAPTER 2

US War Department, FM 31-30, *Tactics and Techniques of Airborne Troops* (1942)

US Military Intelligence Service, *Enemy Air-Borne Forces*, Special Series No. 7 (2 December 1942)

Air Ministry, CD.226, *The Parachute Training Manual* (March 1944) *Accessed at the National Archives AIR 10/3845*

US Military Intelligence Service, 'Rations as a Factor in Paratroop Efficiency', *Intelligence Bulletin* (2 December 1942)

CHAPTER 3

Air Ministry, AP.2097–A P.N., *Pilots Notes for Horsa Glider, with Appendices for Tug Aircraft Pilots* (January 1944) *Accessed at the National Archives AIR 10/2968*

War Office, Army/Air Operations Pamphlet No. 4, *Airborne Airtransported Operations* (1945)

US Army Air Force, T.O. NO 09-40CA-1, *Pilot's Flight Operating Instructions for Army Model CG-4A Glider (British Model Hadrian)* (1942)

CHAPTER 4

Headquarters, No. 38 Wing, 'Tactics adopted for Paratroop dropping' (7 June 1942) *Accessed at the National Archives AIR 39-85*

Air Ministry, CD.226, *The Parachute Training Manual* (March 1944), *Accessed at the National Archives AIR 10/3845*

RAF No. 1 Glider Training School, *Glider Manual* (April 1942) *Accessed at the National Archives AIR 20/6120*

RAF No. 38 Group Headquarters, *Paratrooper and Glider Operations Standard Procedure* (20 July 1945) *Accessed at the National Archives, AIR 20-2011*

CHAPTER 5

US Military Intelligence Service, 'Parachutists (German)', *Intelligence Bulletin* (September 1942)

US Military Intelligence Service, 'Ground Tactics of German Paratroops', *Intelligence Bulletin* (June 1944)

US Military Intelligence Service, 'How Paratroops Clear Fields for Gliders', *Intelligence Bulletin* (June 1944)

US War Department, FM 31-30, *Tactics and Techniques of Airborne Troops* (1942)